What people a ~~~~ the Coronavirus Bible

You get the Coronavirus, you get the Coronavirus, everybody gets the Coronavirus!
Oprah Winfrey[*]

Don't stand so close to me!
Sting (and the Police)

I've never seen another bible like it!
Helen Keller[*]

Brought me closer to God, in a socially distanced manner
Karen

---

[*] Everything's true about these statements except the quotes.

THE
COR🦠NAVIRUS
BIBLE

A PANDEMIC PARODY

Other books by John Spencer

Christian Parody Titles

40 Biblical Ways to Annoy Your Spouse

Not the Christmas Story: A Comedic Christmas Caper

Not the Bible Titles

Not the Parables of Jesus

More Not the Parables of Jesus

Not the Parable of the Good Samaritan

Still More Not the Parables of Jesus

Not the Parable of the Lost Sheep (free for subscribers)

Not the Parable of the Rich Fool (subscribers only)

Not the Christmas Story Vol 1 (with devotional)

Christian Satirical News

The Best of the Salty Cee Vol 1

The Best of the Salty Cee Vol 2

Other books by Paul Kerensa

Noah's Car Park Ark: A Multi-Storey Story

So a Comedian Walks into Church

Hark! The Biography of Christmas

What are they doing down there?

Other books by Church Curmudgeon

Then Tweets My Soul

Other books by Sam Allberry

Why does God care who I sleep with?

7 Myths about Singleness

Connected

THE CORONAVIRUS BIBLE

A PANDEMIC PARODY

John Spencer, David S Smith, Scott Norris
Michael Richard Bullock, et al

Published by:

Kingdom
Collective
Publishing

Unit 10936, PO Box 6945
London, W1A 6US
kingdomcollectivepublishing@gmail.com

Book cover idea by John Spencer, design by Akira
Editing by Katherine.
ISBN: 978-1-912045-80-8

First Edition: April 2020

Dedication

This book is for all those working on the frontlines during this Coronavirus crisis, whether that is through healthcare or supporting those in financial or emotional need.

Charities supported

All proceeds from the sale of this book will be given to the
following faith-based charities working with those in need
during the Coronavirus crisis:

Convoy of Hope

Samaritan's Purse

Restore Hope: Food Box Appeal

The Salvation Army

Genesis 1

The Beginning

In the beginning, the earth was a formless void and darkness covered the face of the deep so as to stop germs spreading.

And God said "Let there be light," and there was light. And God made the light stay two metres away from the darkness. The first day.

And God said, "Let there be a dome in the waters and let it separate the waters above from the waters below," and there was social distancing between bodies of water. The second day.

And God said, "Let dry land appear and bring forth all kinds of vegetation: plants bearing seeds, and fruit and vegetation," for God was stockpiling. The third day.

And God said, "Let there be lights in the sky to separate day from night," because the days were really blending one into another and it was hard to keep track. The fourth day.

And God said, "Let the waters bring forth swarms of creatures: birds and fish both. Let them be fruitful and multiply," for there were no vegetables left on the shelves after the initial panic buying. The fifth day.

And God said, "Let the earth bring forth living creatures of every kind, wild animals and cattle and everything that creeps," because you can only eat fish and poultry so often before it gets repetitive. The sixth day.

And God said, "Let's make man in our own image," because plants and animals just don't have good conversation. God gave the man dominion over all the fish and birds and creatures, but limited him to taking two of each item at a time. The sixth day. Again... For as it stated earlier, the days were merging into one another.

And on the seventh day, God rested at home, as it was the responsible thing to do.

Translator: **Michael Richard Bullock**

Genesis 2

Adam and Eve

Now the LORD God had made a safari park in the east, in Eden; and he put there the man he had formed. And the LORD God made all kinds of animals live there – animals that were easy to catch and tasty to eat. In the middle of the park were the pig of great tasting bacon and the bat of virus creation.

The LORD God took the man and placed him in the Safari Park of Eden to make great barbecues out of the animals there. And the LORD God commanded the man, "You are free to eat any animal in the park; but you must not eat of the bat of virus creation, for when you eat of it you will surely die."

The LORD God quickly noticed the mess that Adam was making in the park and said, "It is not good for man to be alone, I shall make a helper suitable for keeping him in good order."

Now the LORD God brought every beast of the field, birds of the air and fish of the sea to the man and the man named each part of them according to the food he would make of them:

pork, beef, mutton, and venison. But then he ran out of ideas and called chicken chicken and fish fish. However, he did also name the various cuts of them according to their tastiness: loin, spare ribs, bacon, and ham.

Whilst dogs liked Adam and Adam didn't want to eat them, they only added to the mess and so were not a suitable helper. In fact, they only seem to encourage his more base habits.

So the LORD God waited for the man to take another one of his many naps from being tired out after doing so little all day and crafted a woman from one of his spare ribs which therefore would make her simply irresistible to the man.

The LORD God presented the woman to the man. The man said:

"You look a lot like my next wife!"

The woman slapped his presumptuous cheek, but sadly given the lack of anyone else suitable, the woman eventually lowered herself to become his wife.

The man and his wife both wore no personal protection equipment (PPE) and felt no fear.

Translator: **John Spencer**

Genesis 3

The Fall

Now the serpent was craftier that any of the wild animals the LORD God had made. As it was too difficult for the man to catch, Adam never developed a taste for its meat. The crafty serpent said to the woman, "Did God really say, 'You must not eat from any animal in the Wildlife Park?'"

The woman said to the serpent, "We may eat the meat of any animal in the park, but God did say, 'You must not eat the meat from the bat of virus creation, and you must not touch it. Instead, you shall shriek in terror whenever it is used for jump scares in horror movies.'"

"It is not something to be feared but a delicious treat to be consumed!" the serpent said to the woman, "For God knows that when you eat of it the virus will cause your cells to become like God and create many more living beings[2]!"

When the woman saw that the bat was cute and fluffy and good for food, and also desirable for creating something other

---

[2] Well, many more viruses – but this was in the small print that Eve did not check before clicking the "Agree and continue" button.

than the blankets she had made from the animals fur, she took one and threw it on the barbeque and ate it with her husband.

Then the eyes of both of them were opened, and they realised that they weren't wearing any PPE; so they sewed fig leaves together to create facemasks.

Then the man and wife heard the sound of the LORD God as he was walking in the park in the cool of the day, and they kept their distance from him to prevent contagion. But the LORD God called to the man, "Why are you stepping backward as I approach?"

The man answered, "I was practising social distancing to prevent the Coronavirus from spreading between us."

And the LORD God said, "Who told you about social distancing? Have you eaten of the bat of virus creation?"

And the man owned up and said, "Yes I have and I took full responsibility for my actions."

Only joking!

The man blame-shifted like a pro: "That woman you gave to me threw it on the barbeque...and I ate it under protest, for it tasted different to what I am used to."

Then the LORD God said to the woman, "What is this you have done?"

The woman said, "That serpent deceived me from burgers on barbeques and introduced me to all-you-can-eat Chinese bat buffet!"

So the LORD God said to the serpent, "Because you have done this, 'Cursed are you out of all animals for people will now think that you are a scary animal and no longer desire to keep you as a pet[3] you shall now crawl on your belly so you are easy to catch and eat."

To the woman he said, "I will greatly increase your pains by having to home school your kids during quarantine. Also there shall be queues to enter shops and stockpiling shall mean that thy queuing shalt be pointless."

To Adam he said, "Cursed are you to try and work from home with kids distracting you and the internet connection dropping out. There shall now be only one day of the week in your quarantine: Blursday. And because you ate of the bat of virus creation that I forbade you, many of those previously delicious meats will now all taste like chicken to you and you

---

[3] Except for those who have who are showing great depravity because of sin entering the world.

will also have to eat salad as an accompaniment to your meals.

The LORD God made PPE garments of skin for Adam and Eve.

And the LORD God said, "The man is now a virus carrier. He must not be allowed to infect the pig of great tasting bacon and spoil it forever." So the LORD God banished the man from the Safari Park of Eden. And he placed a "Closed because of COVID-19" sign to prevent entry.

Translator: **John Spencer**, with thanks to **Church Curmudgeon** for the Blursday joke.

Genesis 4

Cain and Abel

Adam asked Eve if she wanted to be "known" more deeply in the hope that she would be fooled into thinking this was about talking about deep stuff rather than a Hebrew expression for something else. But she was wise to such schemes. She wasn't exactly in the mood due to the fall.

One day she had a headache, the next day she was too tired, and so on. But Adam was the original inspiration for Jesus' parable of the persistent widow and so kept asking, "C'mon Eve, we're supposed be fruitful and multiply. Remember what happened the last time we disobeyed? We don't want to get cursed again? Besides, since bacon was taken away from us, this is one of the only things that has stayed really great after the curse."

Ever since that fateful day they were expelled from the park, Eve was careful not to be taken in by clever sounding words, although Adam's reasoning seemed sound. Eventually she consented, conceived, and gave birth to Cain.

Eve said, "It's a boy! He's the first human ever born, so I really hope he doesn't grow up to be a murderer or anything like that. That would certainly put my parenting skills in quite a bad light. Just imagine if I was the person he murdered. As it stands right now, there's just me and Adam so I've got a 50/50 chance. For I just love going on the internet and spending hours pondering statistics of my chance of death...and statistics about any catastrophic event that could affect the health of me or my family...or the whole human race."

After seeing how big her belly got with Cain, how uncomfortable and miserable she was during the pregnancy, and how loud she screamed in his face during Cain's birth, Adam was flabbergasted that she was willing to even consider "becoming one flesh" ever again! But statistics told her that having more children would reduce her risk of being murdered and so she was able.

But not being all that good at language arts, she accidentally spelled it wrong, naming her second son Abel.

The Lord asked everyone via voice message to give offerings to Him as an act of worship. So Cain and Abel obliged by setting the items on top of altars. Abel placed ten pristine, fluffy toilet rolls on top of a rock while Cain only gave his used toilet rolls and hoarded the fresh ones for himself!

God looked favourably on Abel's offering[4] but not so on Cain's offering.

Now because Cain relied on his stashed toilet paper to protect him rather than following the protective decrees of the Lord, he soon discovered that he had contracted the Coronavirus unlike his brother Abel.

For in those days, there were plenty of test kits available, for there were only four people on the earth at the time. And the global pandemic internet statistics of cases by nation were really not all that interesting back then - East of Eden: 1, Everywhere else: 0.

After Cain's COVID-19 test came back positive, Cain was very angry, and his countenance fell. So the LORD said to Cain, "Why are you angry? And why has your countenance fallen? You're still young! The mortality rate for people your age is very low. But let this infection be a wake-up call for you to reach out to me in your time of need and follow my commands."

Cain thought about what the Lord had said but then decided against quarantine in favour of taking his brother out for a

---

[4] Because it was a foreshadowing typology of Jesus – the perfect fluffy Lamb of God.

walk before taking him out.

"Let's go out into the field," said Cain, "I must speak with you."

"That's fine, as long as we maintain a distance of at least six feet." Cain was irritated by this regulation.

"I need your help, Abel."

"Wait, I must stop and get the rubber gloves."

"Okay, can we go?!" barked Cain.

"No, I can't find the sanitiser and why aren't you wearing a mask?"

Whilst in the field Cain coughed all over his brother to infect him, but his plans were dashed by Abel's careful use of PPE and so he had to use a rock on his brother's head.

Not the neatest approach, but he was rushed and had to improvise.

Cain hid Abel's body under his giant mound of toilet paper rolls.

God asked Cain "Where is Abel your brother?"

Cain replied, "Am I my brother's keeper?"

God answered, "Well technically yes, as you are keeping his dead body under your bathroom tissue inventory! For the voice of your brother's body cries out to Me from under your Charmin stack!"

"But he can't be crying out to you because I killed him!" said Cain before realising that he had just given the game away.

God said, "Aha! Got you! Anyway, it's just a figure of speech, his body is not ACTUALLY crying out. Don't you know that sometimes I'll be using metaphorical figurative language, at other times narrative or poetry or parables. You have to interpret my words according to the type of language it is – this is basic Bible College stuff."

"Because of what you have done all meat will taste like Brussel sprouts to you and you will be forced to become a vegan."

And Cain said to the LORD, "My punishment is greater than I can bear! Surely You have made me a social media outcast; I shall be hidden, removed from Your Facebook friends list; and it will happen that anyone who finds me on Twitter will troll my feed with taunts about my diet - #Brusselsboy."

And the LORD said, "Not so, if anyone trolls Cain, he will suffer a Twitter ban seven times over." Then the Lord added a coughing gif for Cain's profile picture so that no-one who found him on social media, Skype, Google Hangouts, or Zoom would troll him.

So Cain went out from the Lord's presence and quarantined himself in the land of Nod.

Translators: **David S Smith** and **Scott Norris**

Genesis 6-9
The Flood

The LORD saw how great man's desire was to protest the quarantine and every inclination of the thoughts of his heart was only about purchasing non-essential items and getting haircuts. The LORD was grieved that he had made man on the earth and his heart was filled with pain and his ears were filled with the sound of coughing.

So the LORD said, "I will cleanse the face of the earth with a flood of disinfectant." But Noah found favour in the eyes of the LORD.

So the Lord told Noah to build an ark, which he did or the Bible and indeed all history would have been much shorter.

Then the Lord asked Noah to gather two of each animal out there, one male and one female. Except for chickens, there were to be many of those, as the LORD was preparing the world for the coming glory of Chick-Fil-A.

Every type of animal was to be collected, regardless of whether or not they were clean, unclean, half-clean, ¾ clean, mammal, dinosaur, or insect. Noah immediately sent out an evite via smoke signal and the beasts arrived in an orderly parade.

Though after he started, the Lord said to Noah, "Having just checked the latest guidelines, you're gonna have to double the size of the ark to ensure proper distancing. Also, maybe don't take the bats."

So Noah did as the Lord had commanded but as he was doing so his mind was assailed by the thought of the amount of manure that all these animals would generate and enquired of the Lord, "How will we clean the beasts?"

"I will turn the sap from the ark's wood into sanitiser. Do not doubt my power."

"I will not doubt you, Lord." Immediately after Noah said this, a flock of seagulls dropped an electric washer on the great ship. Noah smiled humbly again and looked excitedly toward the day when electricity would be invented so they could use it. He looked less excitedly at the mop and bucket as the Lord closed the door to the ship.

Disinfectant descended upon the earth for the first and last time ever. The cleansing liquid fell faster than a grocery store shelf of cleaning supplies emptied during a pandemic.

After 40 days, the Lord told Noah to send out a raven and it returned with a few sheets of damp toilet paper that someone had hidden in a tree, a clear sign that the water was receding.

Noah set course to hide the ark so people would speculate for years as to where its final resting place was. Seven days later, he released a dove and it did not return – a clear sign that it had found dry toilet paper to make a nest with.

Noah also realized that he was now the first pirate on earth, which would help impress the ladies should his wife die.

Translators: **Scott Norris, John Spencer** and **Michael Richard Bullock**

Genesis 11
The Tower of Toilet Rolls

Now at that time, all the shops of the world had no restrictions on the number of items purchased.

So, men said to each other, "Come, let's stockpile toilet rolls and build ourselves a tower of them that reaches to the heavens, so that we may make a name for ourselves.

But the LORD came down to see the tower of toilet rolls that the men were building and said, "If they can do this with no restrictions, then nothing will be impossible for them. Come, let us go down and limit the number of essential items they can purchase for themselves."

So the LORD did ensure that Target did place a limit of no more than two toilet rolls per person and the LORD scattered the people all over the earth and ensure that only those of dubious nature did frequent Target thereafter. And that is why the shop was called Target, for it was the target of the LORD's wrath that day and indeed thereafter.

Translator: **John Spencer**

Genesis 17:1-22

God's covenant with Abraham

When Abram was ninety-nine years old, the Lord appeared to him and said, "I am God Almighty, walk before me faithfully and I will make a covenant between me and you."

Abram fell face down, as he wasn't wearing a mask and this was the next best thing, and God said to him, "This is my covenant with you: #1 no longer will you be called Abram, and your wife be called Sarai. For I am blessing you with radically new hip names Abraham and Sarah so you can create new Facebook profiles and get a fresh start."

Abraham said, "But God, they're not really all that different. I mean, Abram-Abraham...Sarai-Sarah. Really? When spoken, I can't even tell the difference between Sarai and Sarah as surely the 'i' at the end is silent. And with my new name, they'll probably just think I've developed a little bit of a stutter in my old age with Abra-[h]-am."

God responded, "Abraham, I need to move this along to the next bullet point in my presentation as I have another meeting to get to, with this troublesome employee named Lucifer who wants me to bring disciplinary action upon another one of my employees named Job, so I'm going to have to ask you to just run with it. OK?"

Abraham was still hung up on the second employee's name, "Wait, you have an employee named Job? He has a job working for you as one of your servants and his name is Job? Is Job his hip new 'original' name you gave him, just like you gave us?"

God ignored Abraham's sarcastic air quotes and petulant line of questioning, "Bullet point #2: Remember, I said you will be the father of a many nations. Well you and Sarah are going to have a son and..."

Then Abraham fell on his face and laughed, saying, "How is that gonna happen? Sarah is 90 years old! We don't ever even 'know' each other anymore!?!"

God tried to encourage Abraham, "Well, your ancestor Adam was pretty active even well into his 800's. And, as you'll see in the future, I don't even need a father to bring forth a child...."

Once Abraham's laughter subsided, God quickly slipped in the last point, "Bullet point #3: The sign of this covenant will involve a little cut."

"A haircut? Well that's no skin off my back!" said Abraham

enthusiastically and became the first person to sign a contract without properly reading the terms and conditions.

Translator: **David S Smith**

Genesis 18:16-19; 19:24-25

Abraham pleads for Sodom and Gomorrah, sort of

Then the LORD said, "The outcry against Sodom and Gomorrah is so great and their sin so grievous that I will go down and see if what they have done is as bad as the outcry that has reached me."

But Abraham approached the LORD and said, "What is their sin that would cause the LORD to go down? Would you sweep away the righteous with the wicked if they were stockpiling toilet paper?"

And the LORD did answer, "For stockpiling toilet paper I would spare the place, but 'tis far worse a crime."

So Abraham did enquire further, "Forgive me for being so bold as to ask, would you sweep away the righteous with the unrighteous if they were failing to flush after a poop."

And the LORD did answer, "For not flushing the toilet, I would spare the place, but 'tis far worse a crime."

Then Abraham said, "May the LORD not be angry, but let

me ask would you destroy the city if the men were leaving the toilet seat up or leaving it down but then peeing all over it?"

And the LORD did reply, "For leaving the toilet seat up or leaving it down and peeing over it, I would spare the city but 'tis far worse a crime."

Then Abraham was stumped and asked, "Forgive me for asking one last time, but what is this outcry so great and this sin so grievous that you would consider sweeping the righteous away with the unrighteous?"

And the LORD with great sadness did reply, "They have been placing the toilet paper under and not over."

And Abraham did grow faint at the mere mention of such a heinous sin and did cry out unto the LORD, "Stuff the righteous – let them all burn!"

Then the Lord rained down many toilet rolls on Sodom and Gomorrah out of the heavens. And those living in the cities used so much toilet paper that they wiped themselves out.

And so Lot's lot in life was to perish in the city of Sodom as an example of what would happen to those who tolerate such unspeakable deviance in their midst.

Translator: **John Spencer**

Genesis 22:1-17

Abraham Tested

Now it came to pass that God tested Abraham, saying, "Abraham!"

And even though Abraham knew not what day it was, he still remembered his name and replied, "Here I am, virus-free by your grace, LORD!"

Then God said, "Well, unfortunately, I'm going to need to change that. For you, Abraham, will develop the full symptoms of COVID-19 and I will cause Isaac to become a high-risk person. Take your son, your only son, Isaac, whom you love to a mountain in the region of Moriah. There you are to cough into the face of your immunocompromised son without either of you wearing any kind of mask."

So Abraham rose early in the morning and travelled to the place God had told him about with Isaac his son.

As they were climbing, Abraham's fever, coughing, and shortness of breath symptoms became obvious to Isaac. Isaac spoke up and said, "My father! It appears that you have the symptoms of COVID-19. Therefore, I must ask you - where is your N95 mask to keep me from contracting this infectious virus?"

Abraham answered, "God himself will provide a mask for my coughing."

Then they came to the place of which God had told him. Abraham felt the tickling in the back of his throat and turned and faced his son.

But the Angel of the LORD called to him from heaven and said, "Abraham, Abraham! Do not spew saliva onto the lad! For now I know that you fear God more than the Coronavirus, since you have not withheld from me your son, your only son."

Abraham looked up and there he saw a shiny brand new N95 mask caught in a thicket by its straps. So Abraham went and took the mask upon his face, protecting his son from his big cough in the face and from further coughing on their return journey. So Abraham named this place "The Lord is my Facemask."

The Angel of the LORD called to Abraham from heaven a second time, and said: "Because you have done this thing, and have not withheld your son, your only son, I will surely bless you. I will rid you of the virus and strengthen your son's immune system and you and your descendants will be at the bottom of the COVID-19 statistics by nation."

Sadly though, God did not ensure that Abraham's mask was free of its unwholesome contents after all his coughing.

Translator: **David S Smith**

Genesis 29:25

Jacob tricked by Laban

And it came to pass, that in the morning, behold, it was Leah...

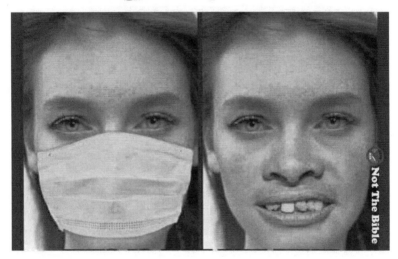

Gen 29:25 (sort of)

And thus was the proverb born: never marry someone in a facemask nor wear a facemask into a bank.

Translator: **John Spencer**

Genesis 41:1-37

Pharaoh's Dreams

We catch up with our hero, Joseph, who was sold into slavery by his brothers, who were jealous of his multi-coloured facemask. Then Joseph was imprisoned after a popular #BelieveAllWomen campaign and an accusation from Potiphar's wife. And finally, after interpreting dreams for Pharaoh's baker and toilet paper bearer there was a rather unexpected two year quarantine before the story progressed further...

Pharaoh had a dream. He was standing by the Nile when out of the river there came up seven (rather soggy) full rolls of three-ply toilet paper. After them, seven (also rather soggy) empty toilet roll tubes came up out of the Nile and stood beside those on the riverbank. And the empty toilet roll tubes ate up the seven full toilet rolls. Then Pharaoh woke up.

In the morning, while Pharaoh was sitting on his "throne", his mind was troubled and he sent for his wise men. He told them his dream but they were unable to interpret it for him. More than likely this was because they were rather embarrassed attending Pharaoh whilst he was on his "throne" in the "smallest room."

However, the toilet roll bearer was used to this sort of thing and was not flustered. He remembered Joseph. So Pharaoh sent for him.

Pharaoh said to Joseph, "I had a dream and no one can interpret it. But I have heard it said that when you hear a dream you can interpret it."

"I cannot do it," Joseph replied to Pharaoh, "but God will hear your ply for help and He will get to the bottom of the problem."

Then Pharaoh said to Joseph, "Your puns are a bit cheeky." And Joseph replied, "I do seem to be on a roll, let's hope it doesn't all go down the tube."

So Pharaoh repeated his dream to Joseph, but we shan't repeat it here to prevent readers from becoming bored. Then Joseph said to Pharaoh, "This is a Charmin dream: God has shown Pharaoh what he is about to do. Seven weeks of great abundance in toiletries are coming throughout the supermarket aisles, but seven crappy weeks of shortages will follow them. Then all the abundance will be forgotten. However, the nagging sense that you shouldn't have executed the baker will only grow."

"I suggest Pharaoh look for a discerning and wise man and put him in charge of the toiletries aisles in supermarkets throughout the land."

"Let Pharaoh appoint restrictions on such products to prevent people from buying more than two items per customer. Let Pharaoh also split three-ply toilet paper into three rolls of one-ply toilet paper as that will create the breakthrough for having enough stock for the crappy weeks."

"Finally, let Pharaoh ensure that all newly built houses come with bidets installed as standard."

"Alternatively, the dream may be the result of eating some bad tacos the night before. In which case, the need for stockpiling toilet paper remains the same."

Then Pharaoh said to Joseph, "Since God has made all these tearable puns known to you and you wisely avoided that dreadful one about Uranus (which won't be discovered for many years hence anyway) there is clearly no one as discerning and wise as you. Henceforth, you shall be placed in charge so that if anything goes wrong I can pin the blame on you and still get re-elected as Pharaoh next year."

Translators: **Church Curmudgeon** and **John Spencer**

Exodus 3:24-25
The Call of Moses

"And an angel of the LORD appeared to him in a flame of fire out of the midst of a bush. He looked, and behold, the bush was burning, but not consumed. And Moses said, "I will turn aside to see this great sight, why the bush is not burned." When the Lord saw that he turned aside to see, God called to him out of the bush, "Moses, Moses!"

And Moses said unto the Lord, "Very impressive and everything, but why the overkill?"

And a voice answered him from the midst of the bush, saying, "I heard you cough as you came and had to be sure you'd keep your distance..."

Then he said, "Now take your sandals off your feet, turn them into a mask, for the place on which you are standing is holy ground and you also rather close still."

And he said, "I am the God of your father, the God of Abraham, the God of Isaac, and the God of Jacob. Join my Zoom conference. The meeting ID is 123-456-789 and the password is Jzus4givz." And Moses hid his face with his sandal mask, for he was afraid to look at God, no matter cough in his presence.

Then the Lord said over the social distancing responsible Zoom conference call, "I have surely seen the affliction of my people who are in Egypt and have heard their cry because of their taskmasters. I know their sufferings, and I have come down to deliver them out of the hand of the Egyptians and to bring them up out of that land to a good and broad land, a land flowing with milk, honey and other essential items that stores are sadly lacking. Alas, Moses could not hear him, as the connection was poor.

But Moses protested, asking, "Who am I to demand this of Pharaoh, he will not listen to me..."

But the Lord reproached him: "I shall mark you as one of my essential workers, entitling you to access to Pharaoh, free parking at the Pyramids, and discounts at the Sphinx coffee shop. Also, all Israel shall stand on the doorsills of their homes and clap for you each and every Thursday at 8 pm"

Translators: **Robbie Squier, Michael Richard Bullock** and **James Grigsby**

Exodus 7:14-12:51

Plagues of Egypt

Moses and Aaron went to Pharaoh and said, "This is what the LORD, the God of Israel, says: 'Let my people go that they may self-isolate in the desert.'"

But Pharaoh's heart was hard, as he had aortic valve calcification due to his diet of bats, which are high in saturated fats. And he said unto Moses, "If you want to isolate so much, then you can make bricks from home without any deliveries of straw."

Moses showed a graph of an exponential curve and replied, "This is what the LORD says: 'At midnight I will go throughout Egypt and every firstborn son will catch COVID-19 and die.'"

And Pharaoh was shocked, "Boy, you really skipped ahead in this whole plagues thing. I thought we'd work through nine others first, but you just went right for the jugular. But the answer is still no."

Then Moses, hot with anger (not with virus symptoms), left Pharaoh.

The LORD said to Moses and Aaron, "If you can work out what day and month it is, then you are to celebrate this day each year as a Passover festival to the LORD. You are to isolate yourself in your houses, have lamb barbeque and coat your doors in essential oils."

"The oil shall be the sign to the angel that your house is a virus-free zone and he will pass over you. Hence, the name Passover. Pretty cool, huh?"

During the night Pharaoh summoned Moses and Aaron and said, "Up! Take your people and socially distance yourself out of here!"

So the Israelites left Egypt, but they didn't walk like an Egyptian as they were Israelites. And also, that would be a rubbish joke based on a naff song from the 80s.

The LORD made the Egyptians favourably disposed towards the Israelites and they gave them as much toilet paper as they asked for.

Translators: **David S Smith, John Spencer, Scott Norris** and **Robbie Squier**

Exodus 14
The Red Sea Crossing

And the Israelites reached the shore where Bo Risjonson meets D'NaldTrumpingtons. And they could hear birdsong, because there were no planes, nor any road traffic, as it was several thousand years ago. But they could hear the hooves and wheels of Pharaohs' chariots and army, as they approachethed. And they could hear the waves, because they were right by the sea, and this beach hadn't been closed as a public space, so that the Israelites could exercise freely for one hour each day.

And some bloke said, "Moses, we'd have been better off staying under Egyptian lockdown than being stuck out here in the wilderness. What were you thinking?" And Moses turned to Aaron for him to answer the question. And Aaron showed them a graph.

So Moses gathered the people and told them, "Do not be afraid." (Which is said a lot throughout the Bible and is a useful thing to remember now and then.) "The Lord God will fight for you, so hold onto your peace. And hold your horses. Well, Pharaoh should." And then he winked, according to reports from someone right at the back who probably couldn't see very clearly.

Then Moses stretched his hand out over the sea, and the Lord God made the sea lift up on either side, parting the waves. And the Israelites breathed a huge sigh of relief, for now there was more room for them to spread out, for the beach was quite tiny and they were risking being quite close together. So they spread out into the space betwixt the waves.

Having held out his hand, Moses then used it to usher the people through with a "Go on then!" And so they did, two metres apart where possible. However, the gap between the waves wasn't vast, so at times they were a little too close, especially when a runner or jogger came past, which was annoying for those walking more slowly. But people looked out for the elderly and infirm, because that's what we do, and always have done, and always will do.

And the Angel of God went behind them and before them as a pillar of cloud by day and a pillar of light by night, showing them the way, at a safe distance. And that bloke again said to Moses, "Are you sure this journey qualifies as essential?" And Moses gestured his thumb behind him and said, "Listen! Do you hear the chariots coming up behind us? I'd say it was pretty essential." And thus Moses tutted.

And lo, the Israelites arrived on a new shore, which surprised them because they didn't know that the borders were open for international travel. They sat on the ground for an all too brief moment as the police moved them on for gathering in a group.

Pharaoh and the Egyptian army approachethed close, having made good time because traffic was light. The Egyptians arrived at the shore where Bo Risjonson meets D'NaldTrumpingtons, and they too embarked across the channel in the sea.

But Moses lowered his hand (having at some point presumably crossed himself), and the waters began to fall. Waves crashed down onto the Egyptians, and they were covered in water, which at least gave the chariots a much-needed deep clean.

But the Israelites were safe, which was all any of them really wanted. They would go on to complain about a lack of food supplies, which would cause manna from heaven, and quail on the ground, and water from a rock, and toilet roll from just behind a big stone, and a few tins of baked beans just inside a cave. And that was when they would realise that their supermarket had delivered and left the bags at a distance from the customers without telling them, so they would have to go on a scavenger hunt to find them. But as scavenger hunts were becoming all the rage it was all a bit of fun while they were on the way to the Promised Land.

For although this was not the Promised Land, it was promising enough. They were just glad to get out of Egyptian lockdown. and this was a good start for now.

Translator: **Paul Kerensa**

Exodus 20:1-17; 24:12

The 10 commandments

And God spoke all these words: "I am the Lord your God, who brought you out of Egypt, out of the land of bat worship and sanitiser shortage.

You shall have no other gods before me. No matter what shortages they say they could end.

You shall not make for yourself any graven image in the form of toilet roll or kitchen towel or any absorbent substance.

You shall not take the name of the Lord your God in vain, no matter how hard you get elbowed in the groin as you reach for the last bag of pasta.

Remember the Sabbath day by keeping it holy. Six days you shall be confused as to the day and wander around the house wearing PJs, but the seventh day is Sabbath to the Lord your God. You shall get dressed and be productive and definitely not use it to queue outside the supermarket because your uncle's cousin's friend said they restocked baked beans.

Honour your father and your mother by telling them to stay safe and stay inside under lock and key as they are vulnerable, so that their days may be long.

You shall not murder, not even to get ibuprofen.

You shall not commit adultery, no matter how hard you're finding 24/7 quarantine with your spouse.

You shall not steal. Not even if you really need those non-essential items that you can't buy.

You shall not give false testimony against your neighbour saying that they broke the lockdown order, even if their music was loud last night, and they still haven't trimmed that tree back.

You shall not covet your neighbour's Netflix subscription, you shall not covet your neighbour's toilet paper, nor his hand sanitiser, nor his PPE, nor his stockpiled food, nor the fact that he's been furloughed and paid but you still have to go to work because Darryl says headaches aren't a symptom of the virus. What does Darryl know anyway?"

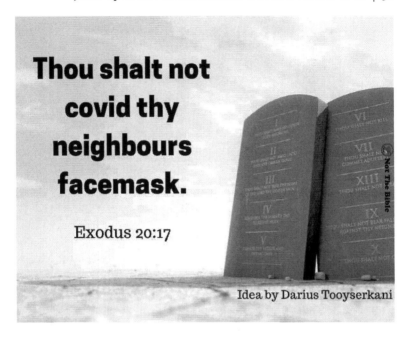

Thou shalt not covid thy neighbours facemask.

Exodus 20:17

Idea by Darius Tooyserkani

Translators: **Michael Richard Bullock, Tristan Searle** and **John Spencer.**

Exodus 32:1-12

The Golden Toilet Roll

The Lord said to Moses, "Come up to Me on the mountain and I will give you tablets of stone with these commandments written so they can be wiped down regularly to prevent infection without becoming faded."

So Moses set out with his Joshua his assistant, and Moses went up on the mountain of God to quarantine with the LORD for 40 days and 40 nights.

The people got impatient waiting for Moses to return from the mountain. So they came to Aaron, and said to him, "Come, let us elect a new government who will end the lockdown so we can purchase non-essentials and have haircuts."

And Aaron said to them, "Technically, we have a theocracy not a democracy, so what you need are new gods not new elected governors. So take off the gold ear-rings that you are wearing and bring them to me. But don't bring me any nose-rings unless they are properly washed first."

Aaron took what they handed him and made it into an idol

cast in the shape of a great roll of toilet paper. Then he said, "This is your god, O Israel, who kept you safe from the Coronavirus."

Aaron built an altar before it. The people rose early on the next day, offered burnt offerings of their stashes of sacred toilet paper. They also engaged in revelry forbidden by the lockdown order, such as gathering in groups of ten or more and dancing without leaving room between them for the Holy Spirit.

Then the LORD said to Moses, "Go down, because your people, whom you brought out of the land of Egypt, have corrupted themselves. For they have made for themselves an idol cast in the shape of a toilet roll, and worshiped it and stockpiled it instead of looking to Me, their true deliverer."

"For they are a stiff-necked people, though to be fair, some of that is because of their unsanctioned dancing. Therefore, let Me alone, that My wrath may burn hot against them and I may consume them like their toilet paper offerings. Then I will make a new great denomination that shuns dancing in favour of pot luck."

Moses was tempted by the pot luck but said, "LORD, please turn from Your fierce wrath and show grace, despite their stupidity for thinking toilet paper can save them from a respiratory condition."

Then the LORD relented and Moses turned and staggered down the mountain with the two tablets of stone.

Joshua took the stone tablets from Moses to prevent the old patriarch from falling. But the ground under Joshua did give way and he slid on his bottom for several hundred cubits.

And Moses did call out with a wry grin, "I'll see you at the bottom then!" And he did make his way down carefully, using his staff. Moses was feeling smug until his staff became a snake and he did tumble too. Thus the ancient but seldom used saying: "Don't lean on sticks that can become serpents".

When they saw wild partying and misbehaviour of all kinds, Moses cried out, "Shut this down," but they did not shut it down. So Moses cried out unto them again, "Shut up," but up they did not shut up either, and one smart Hebrew called Alec replied unto him "Make your mind: shut down or shut up?"

And Moses' anger burned and he hurled the tablets of stone at the Israelites and said, "Take these two tablets and sleep it off!"

And Aaron said, "Do not be angry, my Lord. They got tired of lockdown and were protesting by throwing their ear-rings into the fire when, all of a sudden, this golden toilet roll came out!"

Moses carefully considered Aaron's statement and observed how Aaron's nose grew as he spoke, "Well, I guess it could happen to anyone..."

And the Israelites did promise to never to do such a thing again, or at least until they did again. Whichever came soonest.

So it was as a complete shock when they didn't trust the LORD again as they reached the Promised Land.

Therefore they spent 40 years walking in circles until all their toilet paper was used up. Thus were they forced to depend upon the LORD to cause water to sprout a rock like a primitive bidet.

Translators: **David S Smith, Tim Hill** and **John Spencer.**

Leviticus 13:2-46

The Laws of Moses

When anyone has a new continuous cough or a high temperature, the priest is to examine them, and if it appears they could have the Coronavirus the priest is to pronounce the person unclean and put them in isolation for seven days.

On the seventh day, the priest is to examine them again and if he sees that the symptoms persist; he is to isolate him for another seven days.

On the seventh day, the priest is to examine them once again, and if the symptoms have faded, the priest shall pronounce him clean. He must wash himself in soap and water for at least 20 seconds, and he will be clean.

The person with such an infectious virus must wear pyjamas, let his hair be unkempt, cover the lower part of his face with a mask, and cry out, "Unclean! Unclean!" As long as he has the virus, he remains unclean. He must live alone; he must live outside the camp.

In the distant future shall arise a people who mock these Levitical laws on impurity as cultural, out-dated and barbaric and thus in their wisdom shall the Coronavirus be spread.

Translator: **John Spencer**

1 Opinions 3:6

COVID-19 Guidelines

Current biblical COVID-19 guidelines suggest maintaining a social distance of 300 cubits for 40 days and 40 nights, and washing your hands long enough to recite Psalm 119.

Translator: **Church Curmudgeon**

Leviticus somewhere, honest.

Instructions for Zoom Meetings

These are the regulations for zoom meetings, which are holy unto the LORD:

The priest is to guard the sacred place where the meeting is to be held with a password, and he shall sprinkle its knowledge only to those whom are invited.

And whosoever wouldst partake of the meeting shall consecrate themselves beforehand by covering their nakedness with clothes that are not pyjamas for this is pleasing unto the LORD and to those who might see them.

And whosoever wouldst partake of the meeting shall ensure that they are not disturbed by their spouse, their children, their menservants and maidservants, nor their livestock, cattle, sheep and their asses.

They shalt position themselves not too high so that the hairs of their nostrils are visible, nor too low that only the top of their head is seen. Nor shall they sit wholly to the left, nor to the right but in the centre of the screen shall they place their heads.

And the lighting they shall use must be pleasant unto others: not behind a fan to give seizures to those who observe, nor behind their heads so as to hide their form (unless they be in witness protection).

And the priest shall examine those attendees to ensure they are without spot or blemish of food eating, sniffles or echoes. For such noises down the microphone are an abomination unto the LORD.

And when ye come together, do not be like the Pharisees who shout loudly and ask repeatedly if they canst be heard for they have received their air-time in full. But instead be humble, trust thy microphone icon, mute thy mic when not in use, and speak softly when it is thy turn. For in this way you are sons of the Most High.

And when thou departest from the meeting, take not thy camera with you nor keep thy mic live, for many a man has been humbled by recording that which is better left private.

Translator: **John Spencer**

1 Isolations 24:7

Joshua renews the quarantine

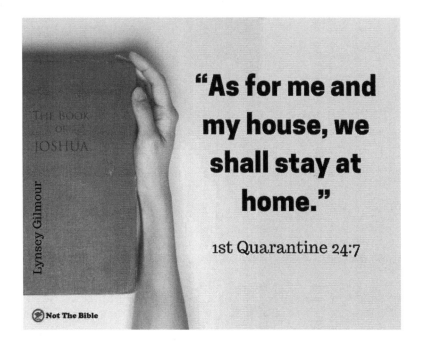

Translator: **Lynsey Gilmour**

Joshua 6

The Battle of Jericho

The Lord spoke to Joshua, telling Him, "Jericho have hoarded toilet roll again. They constantly exceed the one-person shopping rule, and I've seen some of them go out for a run twice a day!"

"But God," said Joshua, "Can't I just rant about it on social media?"

"No, Joshua. You must act!"

Now the gates of Jericho were securely closed as the city was on Lockdown. No-one came in or out, except for their essential journeys. And the people of Jericho believed that they were well isolated behind their giant wall.

Joshua and the army of Israel set out. On their one walk of the day, they walked once around the walls of Jericho, although Captain Tom wanted to do a few more laps. They were wary to maintain the safe-distancing outlined by duct tape lines on the floor. They did this for six days, thus respecting the minimum seven-day quarantine period.

On the seventh day, however, they marched around the walls

seven times. Nevertheless, this was allowed, for they still only exercised once that day and only with members from their household.

And some did say to one another, "Do you feel like we're going around in circles?"

And others did complain of getting dizzy.

But at 8pm they blew loudly on their trumpets and made other such noises in commemoration of the NHS and carers.

And the trumpets did spread the wall demolishing pathogen with greater velocity so that the walls of Jericho fell down, and the Israelites rushed in like shoppers panic buying.

And the toilet roll was spread out equally amongst the people, though some were more equal than others.

Translators: **Israel Matthews, Tristan Searle, Thomas Downs** and **John Spencer**

Judges 7:1-25

Gideon

Gideon and all of the men with him were camped just outside the Midianites encampment, but not close enough to be spotted. They woke up early because that is what biblical heroes do.

Then the Lord said to Gideon, "The people who are with you are too many. They will say that they defeated the Midianites by their own power and not with my help. Send some of them home. Dismiss the ones who are still wearing their PJs when going out in public."

So Gideon sent away the men who were wearing PJs when leaving their homes. 22,000 fighters went home and 10,000 remained.

Then the Lord said to Gideon, "Good work. Now send home the people who don't know what day of the week it is." So, Gideon dismissed all those who had no idea that it was Wednesday and only 300 remained who still knew the day (though admittedly some of those might have just guessed.)

The Lord said to Gideon, "I will deliver you with these 300 men who still have their wits about them despite being in lockdown for months."

So Gideon and his 300 men gathered their provisions and novel trumpets, while the others returned home to their families in holy lockdown.

Now that same night the Lord said to Gideon, "Up, up! Go down to their camp and take it. But if you are afraid, take your buddy Purah with you and spy on them."

So, Gideon and Purah slipped out into the night to observe the enemy. The encampment held not only the Midianites, but also the Coughites, and Feverites, as well as their sons. The enemy were great in number, and their war-camels were sturdy and strong. As Gideon and friend surveyed the enemy, they overheard some loudmouth talking about a dream he had.

"I just dozed off while on duty, so shh, don't tell our leader. But in my dream a golden toilet roll crashed into our camp and flipped our tents over!"

The man next to him was impressed, "That can be nothing other than Gideon, the Israelite." Gideon was so pleased with this news, he decided not to inform their leader of the breach in discipline. Instead, Gideon ran back to camp and prayed to God in thanks, then addressed his troops.

"The Lord will give us victory today! Follow me and do as I do." They slowly made their way to strategic positions outside the enemy base because keeping a distance of six feet made lining up difficult.

Once everyone was finally in position, Gideon gave the signal and each man threw their torches at the enemy's tents while blowing their trumpets! The fires consumed the tents faster than hand sanitiser eats germs. However, the real weapons were those trumpets for they imitated the sounds of constant coughing!

The Feverites screamed, "Coronavirus!" and fled. But the Coughites who used sword jabs to ensure they kept a safe distance from one another soon caused the Midianites to return the jabs with stabs and before long they had turned on each other with their swords.

Gideon sent word of his victory and asked for men from the neighbouring towns to collect the enemy's toilet rolls, all trophies, all for the glory of God.

The following day, Gideon started a new career distributing Bibles throughout the world's hotels and motels.

Translator: **Scott Norris**

Judges 13-16

Samson

Again the Israelites didst evil in the eyes of the LORD, by bowing down to the toilet paper rather than trusting in the LORD for their salvation, so he delivered them into the hands of the Philistines.

An angel of the LORD appeared to a sterile wife of a man named Manoah and said, "You are going to conceive and give birth to a son. No razor is to be used on his head."

The woman asked, "Is he to be a Nazirite?"

The angel replied, "No, it is because he shall be in quarantine from the day of his birth and he will begin deliverance of Israel from the hands of the Philistines."

Some time later, Samson fell in love with a woman whose name was Delilah. This was allowable, as going out of the house to find a wife was considered an essential task in the land.

The rulers of the Philistines went to her and said, "See if you can lure him into showing you the secret of his great strength."

So Delilah said to Samson, "Tell me the secret of your great strength."

Samson answered her, "No razor has ever been used of my head, because I have been quarantined since birth. If my head were shaved, my strength would leave me, and I would become as weak as any other man."

Once he was asleep on her lap, she called a man to shave off the seven braids of his hair.

Then she called, "Samson, the Philistines are upon you!"

But he awoke and beat them all and Delilah said, "You have made a fool of me because you lied to me."

And Samson said, "Sorry about that, I was absolutely desperate for that haircut which is not permitted under the lockdown rules."

"I don't suppose you'll believe me if I say I shall become as weak as any other man if I were to receive a delivery of pasta, eggs, toilet paper and other goods that are scarce because of hoarding?"

Translator: **John Spencer**

1 Samuel 17

David and Goliath

Saul and the Israelites drew up their battle lines on one hill and the Philistines gathered on another, with the valley of Elah between them, which was more than enough to keep them isolated from each other.

A champion named Goliath, who was from Gasp, came out of the Philistine camp. He was over nine feet tall, which meant his head was socially distant from his feet. Now Goliath had a nasty continuous cough. He may have had a fever too, but no-one was tall enough to feel his forehead and check.

Goliath shouted to the ranks of Israel, "Choose a man and have him come down and fight me. *COUGH* If he is able to kill me then *COUGH* we will be your servants; but if I kill him then you will become our servants. *COUGH COUGH*"

Saul and all the Israelites were definitely not terrified and many wanted to go and fight him, but sadly they were in quarantine and were unable to leave their tents. Besides which, fighting was not on the government's list of essential activities, otherwise they would have been there like a shot.

Honest.

For forty days the Philistine came forward every morning and evening and made his coughing known, but the government, well Saul, said that it still wasn't safe to lift the lockdown yet.

Now Jesse sent his son David to his eldest brothers who were camped at the Valley of Elah to take them some fresh new facemasks and surgical gloves.

When he reached the camp, he saw Goliath coughing his usual defiance, along with some rather rude words to describe the cowardice of the Israelites that are best not mentioned.

David asked the men standing near him, "What will be done for the man who kills this Philistine and removes this coughing from Israel? Who is this unmasked Philistine that he should defy the holy lockdown order of the living God?"

What David said was overheard and reported to Saul, and Saul sent for him.

David said to Saul, "Let no-one lose heart on account of this Philistine; your servant will go and fight him."

Saul turned to his servant Bob and said, "Is this true? Are you prepared to fight Goliath?"

Bob looked mortified at the suggestion and so Saul turned back to David, "It appears you are mistaken."

David replied sheepishly, "Well, it was worth a try. I guess I'll have to fight him instead."

Now Goliath wanted to fight with sword and spear, and so Saul dressed David in his own hazmat suit and sword.

"I cannot fight in these because I am not used to them." So David took them off.

"But how will you maintain social distancing rules and fight him?" inquired Saul.

So David took his facemask, sling and five smooth stones from the stream, and approached the Philistine.

Goliath took one look at David and coughed with laughter or laughed with coughter, either way there was much coughing and germs were being spread with abandon.

David reached into his bag and took out a stone, slung it and struck the Philistine on one of his foreheads and Goliath fell face down on the ground.

So David triumphed over the Philistine with a sling and a stone; without breaking the Lord's sacred social distancing directive, he struck down the Philistine and killed him.

And so now it was safe to approach the giant, David donned his surgical gloves and took hold of the Philistine's sword and drew it from the scabbard. And after he killed him, he cut off... well, let's just say that there was no more coughing that day.

When the Philistines saw that the hero was dead, they turned and ran. Coincidentally, at that moment the holy lockdown was lifted and the men of Israel and Judah surged forward with a muffled shout through their facemasks and pursued the quarantine breakers and... well, let's just say that none of them ever did it again.

Translators: **John Spencer, Michael Richard Bullock, Mike Sartoris** and **Zoey Granitz.**

2 Samuel 23:8-23

David's Mighty Men

These are the names of David's mighty men:

Josheb-Basshebeth was chief of the Three; he survived three weeks of quarantine on only one roll of toilet paper.

Next to him was Eleazar son of Dodai who single-handedly flattened the curve with a club.

Next to him was Shammah son of Agee who showered, shaved and dressed every day of the lockdown and even knew which day of the week it was.

During harvest time, three of the thirty chief men came down to David at the cave of Adullam, while a band of Philistines was encamped in the Valley of Rephaim with their garrison at Bethlehem.

David longed for hand-sanitiser and said, "Oh, that someone would get me a bottle of hand-sanitiser from the pharmacy near the gate of Bethlehem!"

So the three mighty men broke through the Philistine lines, queued for 3 hours at the pharmacy without complaining, purchased the over-priced sanitiser and carried it back to

David.

Such were the exploits of the three mighty men.

Abishai the brother of Joab was chief of the Three. He raised his shopping list against three hundred customers, whom he beat to purchase pasta, flour, eggs and toilet paper in one trip, and so became as famous as the Three.

Benaiah son of Jehoiada was a valiant fighter from Kabzeel, who performed great exploits. He washed his hands for three hours solid. He also resisted touching his face for over an hour despite a great itch. Finally, he avoided arguing with his wife during the quarantine by self-isolating in his garden shed. Such were the exploits of Benaiah son of Jehoida; he too was as famous as the three mighty men.

Translator: **John Spencer**

1 Kings 3
The Wisdom of Solomon

And it came to pass that Solomon was promoted to Hospital Administrator, and he went to his new hospital to work but he was inexperienced and so offered up many prayers to God.

The LORD appeared to Solomon in a dream at night: and God said, "Ask! What shall I give you?"

And Solomon said, "O LORD my God, you have made me hospital administrator instead of another, but I am but a recent college graduate: I know not how to run a hospital!

"And your servant is in the midst of a global pandemic, a great illness, and patients are too numerous to be numbered nor can projections be trusted for reliability.

"Therefore give your servant an understanding heart to judge our staff that I may discern between good and bad: for who is able to judge so many employees?"

The speech pleased the Lord and so God said unto him, "Because you have asked this thing, and have not asked for a hedge of face mask protection for yourself, nor for many toilet rolls for hoarding, but have asked for yourself understanding to discern judgement; behold, I have given you a wise and understanding heart; so that there has never been a hospital administrator like you before, nor shall any hospital administrator like you come after which kind of explains why things have gone downhill since."

And Solomon awoke; and, indeed, it had been a dream. And he came to the hospital and stood before his staff providing N95 masks to all his employees.

Then came two women, both nurses, unto the Hospital Administrator, and stood before him.

And the one nurse said, "Sir, this nurse and I work in the same ward; and both of us were provided with a ventilator. And we worked together; there were no other nurses on duty with us in the ICU, save we two in ward.

"And this woman's ventilator broke during her rounds; because she is careless.

"And she approached mid-shift, and took my ventilator from my office, while I treated a patient, and laid her broken ventilator in its place.

"And when I plugged in my ventilator to treat a sick patient it was broken but when I examined it closely in the morning, I saw it was not my ventilator which I had been issued."

And the other nurse said "No! The functioning ventilator is mine, and the broken one is your ventilator." But the first one insisted, "Tis not and you're a big fat liar."

And the other did reply, "Who are you calling fat?" And so they argued before the hospital administrator.

And the administrator did develop one of those splitting headaches that were all too common for one in his role.

And the hospital administrator said, "Bring me a baseball bat." And an intern brought a baseball bat before his boss.

And the hospital administrator said, "Smash the functioning ventilator in two, and give half to the one nurse, and half to the other."

Then the nurse whose ventilator was functioning spoke to Solomon, for her heart yearned with compassion for her patients, "O boss, give her the working ventilator, and in no way destroy it."

But the other said, "Let it be neither mine nor hers, but smash it!"

So the hospital administrator answered and said, "Give the

first nurse the functioning ventilator, and in no way damage it: for she is the better nurse."

When all the hospital staff heard the verdict the administrator had given, they held him in awe, because they saw that he had wisdom from God to lead them through this unprecedented crisis and ensure that essential workers had working equipment.

Translator: **Richie Richards**

1 Kings 17:13-14

Elijah and the Widow

**Elijah said to her, "Don't be afraid...
The toilet roll will not be used up and the
handsoap will not run dry until the day the
Lord releases you from quarantine."**

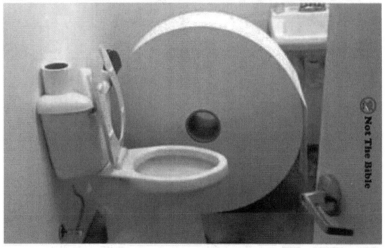

1 Kings 17:13-14 (updated)

Translator: **John Spencer**

2 Kings 6:17

Elisha is surrounded

But Elisha's servant would not
wash his hands nor wear a mask...

**And Elisha prayed, "Open his eyes,
Lord, so that he may see the virus."**

2 Kings 6:17 (sort of)

Translator: **John Spencer**

Psalm 20

A Psalm of David

Some trust in lysol and some in toilet roll, but we trust in the name of the Lord our God....

Ps 20:7 (sort of)

Translator: **John Spencer**

Psalm 23

The Lord is my Sales Assistant

The Lord is my Sales Assistant, I shall not want,

He maketh me to stay a safe distance from other shoppers,

He leadeth me to stocked shelves.

He restoreth my health, he leadeth me in the ways of hygiene: singing Happy Birthday as I scrubbeth.

Yea, though I walk through the valley of stockpiling, I shall not panic buy, for thou art with me and thy online delivery system comforteth me.

Thou prepareth a table of canned goods before me, my trolley runneth over.

Surely soap and water will follow me all the days of my life and I shall dwell in the quarantine of your house forever.

Translator: **Michael Richard Bullock**

Psalm 121

A Song of Ascents

I lift up my eyes to the stockpiling; where does my help come from? Not from 300 rolls of toilet paper (twin-ply), but from the Lord; the Maker of heaven, earth and hand sanitiser.

He will not let your hand go unwashed; he who cleanses you will not slumber;

Indeed, he who watches over all self-isolating; will both cleanse and rinse.

The Lord protects you; the Lord is the antibacterial wipe in your right hand;

The cough will not harm you by day; nor the sneeze by night (bless you), as long as you catch it, bin it, and kill it.

The Lord, and increased personal hygiene, will keep you from all harm; he will watch over your trips to the supermarket (max 2 items);

The Lord will watch over your washing and drying; both now and forevermore.

Translator: **Pete Hawkins**

Proverbs

The Proverbs of Solomon

Proverbs 3:5-6

Trust in the Lord with all your heart and lean not on your own understanding of the Government's Press Conference

In all your quarantining acknowledge him and he will make your curves straight – well flatter.

Proverbs 9:10

The fear of the Lord is the beginning of wisdom and knowledge on the two metre rule, tolerating family members and how to set up Zoom calls.

Proverbs 14:26

He who fears the virus will hide in a secure fortress.

And for his children it will be a refuge...well, maybe more like a prison.

Proverbs 13:12

The quarantine end deferred makes the heart sick but a haircut appointment fulfilled is a tree of life.

Proverbs 15:1

A gentle mask turns away infection. However, inaudible, muffled talking from behind a PPE mask stirs up annoyance

Proverbs 16:18

Pride goes before destruction and the spirit is dampened by too much Netflix

Proverbs 15:3

The eyes of the police are everywhere (well mostly parks and beaches) keeping watch over those who break the quarantine.

Proverbs 15:30

A cheerful look brings joy to the heart, and good news gives health to the bones which is why we're feeling so miserable at the moment.

Proverbs 18:24

A man of many companions may come to ruin because there is a virus who sticks closer than a brother

Proverbs 21:9

Better to break the quarantine than share a house with a quarrelsome wife.

Proverbs 21:23

He who guards his mouth and tongue keeps himself from infection

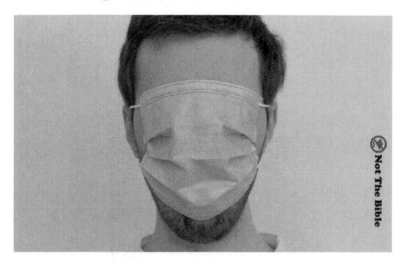

Proverbs 21:23
(sort of)

Proverbs 22:6

Train a child up in the way he should quarantine and when he is a teenager he will not depart from his room.

Proverbs 24:26

An honest answer is like a kiss on the lips. So dishonesty is your best bet to reduce the chance of infection.

Proverbs 25:28

Like a city whose walls are broken down is a man who lacks PPE.

Proverbs 26:11

As a hand returns to touch its face so a fool repeats his folly.

Proverbs 27:1

Do not boast about tomorrow, for you do not know what day it is today.

Proverbs 27:6

PPE from a friend can be trusted, but an enemy multiplies kisses, handshakes, and other contact.

Proverbs 29:18

Where there is no lock on the fridge the people cast off restraint but blessed is he who doesn't eat all his stockpiled food.

Proverbs 30:15b-16

There are three things that are never satisfied, four that never say, 'Enough!':

the replaying of the same song on K-LOVE,

the offense taken by the Millennials,

televangelists which are never satisfied with donations,

and people receiving stimulus cheques, who never say, 'Enough!"

Proverbs 31:6-7

Give beer to those who are in self-isolation, wine to those who are in lock down. Let them drink and forget their quarantine and remember their misery no more

Translators: **John Spencer** and **Bentley Browning**

Proverbs 31
The wife of noble character

Who can find a virtuous infection-free wife?

For her worth is far above toilet paper.

Her hand-sanitized husband safely trusts her; so he will never get the virus.

She empties the grocery store shelves all the days of the pandemic.

She seeks paper products, and willingly works with essential oils to bring her homemade hand sanitiser recipe to the merchant ships while maintaining social distancing protocols.

She ships her food from Amazon to avoid any added social contact.

She also rises while it is yet night to keep tabs on the COVID-19 infection statistics in various states and countries.

And provides food for her household because all the restaurants are closed.

And fires her maidservants since, who knows, they might be carriers!

She considers stock in Scott Paper Company and buys it.

From her profits she increases her homemade hand-sanitiser production quotas to meet demand.

She perceives that her essential oils and alcohol content are both good.

She girds herself with a stylish N95 mask.

And her internet connection does not go out by night.

She puts her hand to the spindle to make cloth in case paper products do end up running out.

She extends her hand to wipe horizontal surfaces that are in need of daily doses of disinfecting.

She is not afraid of visitors to her household, for all her household is also clothed with N95 masks...but turns them all away anyway, just to be extra safe.

Her husband is known throughout the land for selling toilet paper on the black market as he sits among the preppers of the land.

Paranoia and precaution are her clothing; she shall rejoice when the time of COVID-19 has come and gone.

She opens her mouth with wisdom for how to prepare for

catastrophes and on her tongue is the fine print within the governor's "shelter-at-home" laws.

She watches over the driveway of her household to shoo away any and all visitors.

And does not wash her hands with idleness but with THREE Happy Birthday recitations.

Her children rise up and call her blessed and Corona-free.

Her husband also, and he praises her: "Many preppers have done well, but you excel them all."

CNN is deceitful and Trump is passing, but a woman who fears the LORD and COVID-19, she shall be praised."

Translator: **David S Smith**

Ecclesiastes 3:1-8
A Time for Everything

There is a time for everything and a season for every quarantine activity under heaven:

A time to embrace and a time to social distance;

A time to repeatedly touch your face and a time to refrain;

A time to know what day it is and a time to wander in a haze;

A time to stay in your day pyjamas and a time to change into night pyjamas;

A time to do activities with your children and a time to hide away from them in the loft/car/bathroom;

A time to wave at the neighbours in a friendly way and a time to shut the windows and moan about them;

A time to leave the house on an essential journey and a time to just move to a different room for variety;

A time to hoard toilet paper and a time to give to those in need;

A time to do those odd jobs around the house and a time to lie on the sofa complaining;

A time to reflect on your life and a time to social distance from yourself;

A time to wash your hands for 20 seconds and a time to give a quick rinse and dry them on your trousers;

A time to do an online workout and a time to binge on Netflix;

A time to read a book and a time to read a book;

A time to obsess over endless news feeds and panic and a time to switch them all off and trust God.

Translators: **David S Smith** and **John Spencer**

Song of Songs 1:1-17

Solomon's Song of Songs

The Song of Corona, which is a global pandemic

Let him wave to me from a distance – for your distance is more delightful than infection.

Pleasing is the fragrance of your hand sanitiser; your name is like Lysol® poured out. No wonder the virus hates you!

Let me Zoom with you – let us hurry! Let the internet bring me into his chambers. We rejoice and delight in you; we will praise your isolation more than wine. How right they are to adore you!

In quarantine am I, yet lovely, daughters of Jerusalem, lonely like the celebrities in their mansions with no attention.

Do not stare at me because I have been in pyjamas for 14 days, because I have not put on any makeup. My mother's sons were angry with me and made me take a shower; my own vineyard I had to neglect.

Tell me, you whom I love, where you get your bread and toilet paper? Why can't I find any anywhere?

If you do not know, most infected women, follow the CDC guidelines.

I liken you, my darling, to an Amazon Prime delivery driver bringing me parchment to cleanse my quarters.

Your fever is high and your cough is alarming.

We will make you go to the hospital soon if this does not clear up.

While the president was at his table, my Lysol did more work.

My infected is to me a sachet of death resting between my breasts.

My infected is to me a cluster of germ blossoms from the vineyards of China.

How sick you are, my darling! Oh, how sick! Your eyes are bloodshot.

How sick you are, my beloved! Oh, how sick! And our hospital bed is occupied.

The beams of our *COUGH COUGH COUGH COUGH COUGH*.

Translator: **The Church News Headlines**

Daniel 6:10-28
Daniel and the Lions' Den

How lions prey during lockdown:

Dan 6:17
(coronavirus bible version)

Translator: **John Spencer**

Jonah 1:1-4:11

Jonah

Now the word of the Lord came to Jonah and said, "Go at once to Nineveh, the great city, and cry out against it, for their quarantine breaking wickedness has come up before me."

But Jonah had a persistent dry cough and so went to Joppa to self-isolate. However, prophets were classed as essential workers and since it was not possible for him to work from home, the Lord told him to continue to Nineveh anyway.

Jonah knew how vast a city was Nineveh, and how tightly packed its citizens were, and so he boarded a ship sailing away from Nineveh. He went down to the deepest parts of the ship to self-isolate. God sent a storm to hit the ship and the captain commanded Jonah, even though the prophet had a cough, to get on deck.

When it was discovered that several sailors had pre-existing conditions, they decided to throw Jonah overboard. The Lord appointed a fish to swallow Jonah and he spent 3 days in the belly of the fish: far short of the recommended 7-14 day isolation period.

The fish spat Jonah out near Nineveh and he travelled into the heart of the city. This was classed as non-essential travel but the Lord said if Jonah was stopped by a Ninevite police officer, Jonah should put on a sweatband and state he was doing his daily exercise.

When Jonah reached the king he spluttered: "Yet three *cough* days and *cough* Nineveh will be *cough* overturned." With the number of people he had passed enroute and with an understanding of the mathematics behind exponential growth, his prediction was fairly solid.

When the king heard this, he stepped off his throne, threw himself down into the dust, and tore his clothes. The latter was because he was overweight, rather than a deliberate act.

The king issued a proclamation for the city to repent of their irresponsible ways, starting with flushing the toilet and the washing of their hands after they'd been to the bathroom.

When God saw what they had done and how they turned from their evil ways, he relented and did not bring on them the destruction he had threatened.

After three days, like manna from heaven, ventilators, surgical masks, and vaccines fell upon the people of Nineveh and the city was spared.

But Jonah coughed angrily. "Woah, I'm *cough* a frontline worker *cough* and I never even got tested..."

Jonah went to a nearby hill to finally self-isolate responsibly. He grumbled about the lack of a toilet roll and the Lord appointed a bidet to sprout up out of the ground for Jonah. At first, he had no idea what it was but after some experimenting he discovered how superior it was in comparison to the toilet paper he had first longed for.

The next day, the Lord caused a drop in water pressure to stop the bidet from working and Jonah complained, "It is better for me to die than to resort to wiping my behind with paper again."

But the Lord said, "You are concerned about this bidet, though you did not make it nor realise at first how superior it was to toilet paper. Should I not have concern for the city of Nineveh in which there are more than a hundred and twenty thousand people who cannot tell the difference between washing their hands properly and just putting them under water and wiping them on their trousers?"

Translators: **Michael Richard Bullock** and **John Spencer**

Matthew 1:18-22

Birth of the Coronials

Now the birth of "Coronials" took place in this way:

When their parents had been sheltering-in-place for many weeks, the wife was found to be with child because there was not much else to do. And her husband, worried about raising a child during this volatile economic time, thought about putting the child up for adoption.

But as he thought about these things, behold, an angel appeared to him saying, "Mister, do not fear to raise this child, for what is conceived is from 2020. Your wife will bear a child, and you shall call their generation 'Coronials' for they were conceived during the social distancing."

All this took place to fulfil the need for a generational name after Gen Z.

Translator: **The Satire Bible**

Matthew 3

John the Baptist

In those days, John the Baptist came preaching in the wilderness as he was the most lit of all social distancers.

He came in the spirit of Elijah, who ~~ran and hid~~ social distanced from Jezebel. John's clothes were made of camel hair, which doubled as a substitute for toilet paper should the Romans or Jews have hoarded all the rolls at the local market.

People went out to John from Jerusalem and Judea and the whole region of the Jordan. John not only kept them more than six foot away but also had them wash for more than 20 seconds in the waters of the Jordan just to be safe.

They confessed to making excuses to break the Lord's holy lockdown for non-essential journeys, including travelling to this wilderness instead of tuning into his live-stream broadcast at home.

John continued, "I make sure you wash with soap water to kill the virus. But after me comes one more powerful than I, whose facemask straps I am not worthy to tie. He will cleanse you with hand-sanitiser and, should that fail, fire. His bleach spray gun is in his hand, and he will cleanse all surfaces from their germs, sending them into oblivion where they belong!"

Then Jesus came into John's live-stream from Galilee and asked to be washed by John. John tried to deter him, saying, "It's not something I can do remotely via the internet."

Jesus replied, "Then use an electric water pistol or post some soap and water to me." Then John consented.

As soon as Jesus was baptised, he went out of the water (otherwise he would have drowned) and heaven was opened and the Holy Sanitiser descended upon him like a great dollop of ice-cream.

Then a voice from heaven said something which wasn't heard by others as Jesus was in isolation until his essential ministry began.

Translators: **Scott Norris** and **John Spencer**

Matthew 4:1-11
The Temptation of Christ

Jesus, full of the Holy Spirit, and seven bottles of sanitiser, left his home and was led by the Spirit into the wilderness for extended social distancing. He was told that it was an essential service and He had to go.

After being quarantined for forty days and forty nights with no food, he was both hungry and ready to go out.

The devil said to him "If you are the Son of God, order these stores to be full of bread and flour."

Jesus answered, "It is written: 'Man shall not live on bread alone, as tacos and pizza are excellent alternatives.'"

The devil led him to Jerusalem and had him stand in the most crowded place of the temple. "If you are the Son of God, though mortal,' he said, "cough onto everyone here. For it is written, 'The Lord is with them; they will not be afraid. What can mere mortals do to them?'"

Jesus answered, "It is said 'Do not put the Lord your God to the test.'"

The devil led him up to a high place and showed him in an

instant all the kingdoms of the world. And he said to him, "I will give you all their authority and splendour; it has been given to me, and I can give it to anyone I want to. If you shake my hand, it will all be yours."

Jesus answered: "Be gone! For it is written by various health experts, 'Wash your hands, avoid physical contact with others, and keep two metres away!'"

Then Satan left him, and behold, probiotics came and strengthened him.

Jesus returned to Galilee, fully sanitized, in the power of the Spirit, and news about him spread like coronavirus through the countryside.

Translators: **Filbert Joshua, The Satire Bible, Zach Brenner** and **Rachel Louise**

John 2:1-12
Jesus turns water into sanitiser

A wedding took place in a large open space in Cana in Galilee to keep people at an appropriate distance apart[5]. Jesus' mother was there, and Jesus and his disciples had also been invited. When all the hand sanitiser was gone, Jesus' mother said to him, "They have no more hand sanitiser!"

"Woman, why do you involve me?" Jesus replied.

And his mother answered him thus, "Because if you don't help, they won't be able to serve tacos."

So Jesus said to the servants, "Fill those huge jars with water" and they did so.

Then he told them, "Now scoop some out and take it to the head chef."

They did so, and the head chef saw the cleanliness of his hands, smelt the heavenly fragrance of the sanitiser, and noted the moisturising nature that left his hands feeling soft and supple.

---

[5] Except, obviously, the bride and groom after they were married.

He said, "Everyone usually brings out the best sanitiser first and then fills up those expensive looking bottles with the cheap stuff from Walmart when no-one cares anymore because their hands are so chapped from washing. Yet, you have saved the best until now!"

What Jesus did in Cana of Galilee was the first of the signs through which he revealed his glory; and his disciples believed in him. But not enough to stop filling their pockets with the stuff in case it ran out.

Translator: **John Spencer**

Luke 4:16-19

Jesus at Nazareth

He went to Nazareth, where he had been quarantined as a child, and on the Sabbath day he joined the synagogue zoom meeting and read:

"The Spirit of the LORD is upon me,

Because he had anointed me with sanitiser

To deliver food parcels to the poor.

He has sent me to proclaim freedom for those quarantined

and recovery of breath for those struggling

to release those that are oppressed by being stuck in

to proclaim the year of the LORD's favour."

Translator: **John Spencer**

John 3:5-8

Jesus and Nicodemus

Jesus answered, "Most assuredly, I say to you, unless one is born of social-distancing and hand sanitiser, he cannot be safe from the Coronavirus. That which is born of covid-19 is covid-19; and that which is born of anything else could also be covid-19. Do not marvel that I said to you, 'You must be shut in for many weeks.' The sneeze blows where it wishes, and you hear the sound of it, but cannot tell where it comes from and where it goes. So it is with the oft asymptomatic Coronavirus."

Translator: **Othniel Downs**

John 4:6-15

Jesus & the Woman at Costco

Jesus, tired from his travels, went into Costco just before closing. A woman pushing an empty cart passed by him.

Jesus asked her, "Woman, why is your cart empty?" She said to him, "Do you not know, all the toilet paper in the region is gone?"

Jesus answered her, "If you knew the power of God, and who you were talking to, you would have asked him, and he would have given you the roll that never ends."

The woman responded, "Sir, you have no cart and the store is empty, where do you have the roll that never ends? Are you greater than the manufacturers? They produce the toilet paper and distribute it to us."

Jesus said to her, "Everyone who uses their toilet paper will run out and must brave the crowds again. The toilet paper I give will keep unravelling forever."

The woman said, "Sir, give this roll to me, so that I will not run out then have to brave the store and risk infection!"

Translator: **The Satire Bible**

John 5:2-12

The Healing at the Pool

Now there is in Jerusalem by the Sheep Gate a quarantined pool, which is called in Hebrew, Bethesda, having five porches.

In these lived a great multitude of sick people, blind, lame, paralysed, and coronavirus infected, waiting for the delivery of toilet paper.

For an angel went down at a certain time and gave out toilet paper; then whoever got there first received toilet paper and was made well of whatever disease he had.

Now a certain man was there who had coronavirus symptoms and had been isolating for thirty-eight years. When Jesus saw him overweight, lying there on the sofa in his stained pyjamas not knowing what day of the week it was, he knew that he had been quarantined a long time.

Jesus said to him, "Do you want to be set free from the quarantine?"

The sick man answered him, "Sir, I have no man to fetch me toilet paper when the angel distributes it: for I cannot break quarantine and infect others. So another always gets the toilet paper before me.

Jesus said to him, "Rise, purchase a bidet and wash. And immediately the man was made well, and purchased a bidet, and washed"

But the people who saw him said, "It is not lawful for you to buy...whatever that is, as it's not an essential purchase!"

Translator: **Othniel Downs**

Matthew 5:1–12
The Beatitudes

Now when Jesus saw the crowds, he went up on a mountainside and told them to disperse, else they be fined.

His disciples came to him and, sitting them at least two metres apart, he began to teach them. He said:

"Blessed are the hospital NHS staff, for theirs is an unenviable task.

Blessed are the care givers, for they will be a comfort to those whom they serve.

Blessed are the essential workers, for they will keep eggs, flour and pasta on the shelves.

Blessed are those who hunger and thirst, for they are surely the ones only buying supplies when they need.

Blessed are those that queue properly, for they are showing patience.

Blessed are those with a Netflix account, for their password is of more value than gold.

Blessed are the bread maker machines, for they have finally

been dragged out from the back of the larder.

Blessed are those who wash their hands, keep their distance, and persevere during lock-down, for theirs is the moral high-ground."

"Blessed are you when people Facetime, Skype or Zoom chat you, as it shows they are missing spending time with you because of COVID-19. Rejoice and be glad, because great will taste your first pint once the pubs reopen."

Translators: **Pete Hawkins** and **Patience Domowski**

Matthew 5:21-42
The Sermon on the Mount 1

Murder

"You have heard that it was said to people long ago, 'You shall not murder. Whosoever murders will be subject to judgment.' But I tell you that anyone who is angry with a brother or sister will be subject to judgement. This will mean absolutely everyone who been in quarantine with their family is in big trouble."

"Settle matters quickly with your adversary who is taking you to court. Do it while you are still together on the way, making sure to project your voice so you can be heard from at least six feet away! Do this or your adversary may send you to prison. Given the rate at which the government is releasing criminals every day to stop the coronavirus, it probably won't be that bad."

Translator: **Scott Norris**

Judgement

"You have heard that it was said, 'There's no confirmed cases in your region.' But I tell you, anyone who has given dirty glances to those with seasonal allergies has already committed Corona judgement in his heart."

"If your right hand touches a surface, wash your hands, for it is better that your hands get cracked and dried than for your whole body to get Coronavirus. And if your right eye itches, hold that itch, for it is better to suffer an itchy eye than for your whole body to suffer through Coronavirus."

Translator: **The Satire Bible**

An Eye for an Eye

You have heard that it was said, 'A cough for a cough and a sneeze for a sneeze. But I tell you, do not resist shaking hands with an evil person while avoiding touching your face until you have washed your hands for at least 20 seconds.

If someone slaps you on the right cheek, offer them the other cheek. Then go home with them and isolate together until the shelter-in-place conditions have lifted. You have made a new friend.

If someone covets your toilet rolls, give to them your hand sanitiser also.

Give to the one that asks of you and do not turn away the one who wants to borrow from you, as long as they stand at a distance until you have placed the item outside of your house and returned to where you came.

"If anyone forces you to wear one mask, go wear two masks for them."

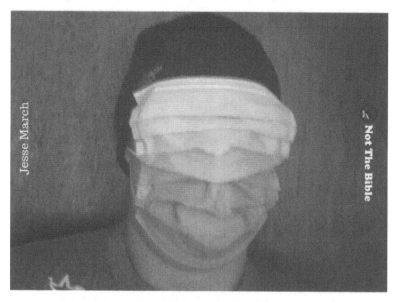

Matt 5:41 (sort of)

Translators: **Scott Norris, John Spencer, Cheryl Booker** and **Jesse March**

Matthew 6:5-15
The Lord's Prayer

"And when you wash your hands, do not heap up empty phrases as the government had recommended, like happy birthday, or those other silly instruction memes going around with various lyrics to sings to ensure you wash your hands for a good amount of time. They think that they are entertaining but they are actually confusing for their many words. Do not be like them, for your Father knows what you need before you ask him. Wash your hands while praying like this:

Our Father, who art a minimum of 6 foot away, how sterile be thy name

Thy Kingdom come (within appropriate delivery times, standing a safe distance away from the door), Thy Will be done, in my home because I can't go out.

Give us today, whatever day this is, a home delivery slot for our daily bread and toilet paper,

And forgive us our messy hair, while we forgive those wearing the same pyjamas for a week.

*And lead us not outside into contamination, but deliver us
from cabin fever and binging on Netflix*

For Thine is the Kingdom, the sanitiser, and the PPE,

For all of Lockdown (which feels like forever and ever)

A-choo

And then use moisturiser so your hands don't dry out."

Translators: **Toby Isaacson, Mike Sartoris, Josh Fitkin, Israel
Matthews, Nathan Ramsden-Lock**

Matthew 6:16-7
The Sermon on the Mount 2

Quarantining

"When you quarantine, do not be like those who wear the same pyjamas and let their hair grow long and unkempt and then eat all their stockpiled food to show others how they are suffering. Truly I tell you, they have received their reward in full. But when you quarantine, put on fresh clothes, brush your hair, and eat sensibly, and your Father, who sees you quarantining in secret, will reward you by allowing your clothes to still fit at the end of your quarantine"

Translator: **John Spencer**

Treasures in Heaven

Do not store up for yourselves treasures on earth...

Matt 6:19 (sort of)

Translator: **John Spencer**

Do Not Worry

Then Jesus said to his disciples: "Therefore I tell you, do not worry about your life, what you will eat; or about your body, what you will wear.

For the pagan world runs after all such things, and wasteth hours queuing outside the local supermarket for the non-existent stocks that the stores promiseth. Your Father knows that you need these things, so instead sit back, relax, and attendeth an online prayer meeting and the Lord will provide in an appropriate manna.

Translator: **Nathan Ramsden-Lock**

Ask, seek, knock

And Jesus said to them, "Which of you, if you go to a friend at midnight, and say, 'Friend, lend me three rolls of toilet paper, for a friend of mine has come to me from a journey, and I have nothing for him to wipe his behind with,' and he will answer from within, 'Don't bother me. The door is now shut, and my children are with me in bed. I cannot get up and give you anything'? I tell you, although he will not rise and give it to him because he is his friend, yet because of his friend's persistence, he will get up and give him as many rolls as he needs."

Translator: **Tim Chase**

The wise and foolish builders

Everyone who says he hears these words of mine and puts them into practice is probably a liar as it's much easier just to talk about it or point at others who aren't doing the parts that you are doing.

However, everyone who hears these words of mine and does not put them into practice is like a man who stockpiles toilet paper for a respiratory condition.

Translator: **John Spencer**

Luke 10:25-37

The Good Social Distancing Samaritan

A lawyer, desiring to justify himself, said to Jesus, "And who is my neighbour?"

Jesus replied, "A man was going down from Jerusalem to Jericho on his daily 30 minute jog/shop for essentials. He fell among robbers, who were struggling due to the amount of occupied houses reducing their burglary opportunities. They stripped him, beat him then departed, leaving him half dead."

"Now by chance a priest was going down that road, and when he saw him he passed by on the other side at the distance of two meters. Likewise a Levite, when he came to the place and saw him, passed by on the other side."

"But a Samaritan, as he was heading to buy essentials also, including groceries to drop off for his elderly mother, came to where he was, and when he saw him, he had compassion."

Choose your own ending:

Ending 1: The Samaritan helps out

"The Samaritan went to him and bandaged his wounds, pouring on oil and wine. Then he put the man on his own donkey, brought him to an inn and took care of him. The next day he took out two denarii and gave them to the innkeeper. 'Look after him,' he said, 'and when I return, I will reimburse you for any extra expense you may have.'

Which of these three do you think was a neighbour to the man who fell into the hands of robbers?"

The expert in the law replied, "The one who had mercy on him."

Jesus told him, "No! It was the priest and the Levite! They were adhering to the 6-foot social distancing. That's why the coronavirus was really bad in Samaria. Follow the government guidelines like the priests and the Levites do!"

Ending 2: The Samaritan helps out wearing PPE

"He donned his face mask and latex gloves and went to him and bound up his wounds, pouring on oil, wine and anti-bacterial alcohol rub. Then he set him on his own animal and brought him to an inn. But the inn was closed following government guidelines. This put the Samaritan in quite a predicament. He couldn't take the man to his mother's place. That would put her at risk. He couldn't turn around, otherwise his mother wouldn't have the needed groceries. After some dithering, the Samaritan decided not to take care of him after all, mumbling something about, 'the greater good'. And the next day on his way back he found the man there, who had not yet succumbed to his injuries.

"'Good to see you again!' said the Samaritan. He took out two denarii and gave them to the man, saying, 'Hopefully you can finish your shopping now.' "

"Which of these three, do you think, proved to be a neighbour to the man who fell among the robbers?"

The lawyer said, "The priest or the Levite because they adhered to the government advice on social distancing and thus flattened the curve?"

And Jesus said to him, "No you dense buffoon. I've been

trying to say this for weeks. Law keeping isn't as important as compassion."

"Yes," said the lawyer, "but surely in these times we have to be wise as well as compassionate and I do think the priest staying away from the unclean was...." He trailed off.

Jesus gave him that look he was known to give many a pharisee.

"I know we're in uncertain times," said Jesus. "But we have to stay compassionate and not be slaves of fear." Jesus looked directly at Mark, who had been recording events, as if to acknowledge this would later become a key section of a hit single that would likely win a dove award or something.

"Don't just hide away safe in your house! Prayerfully consider how you can do more to support those in need."

Jesus' disciples were stunned. This was the first time, in their estimation at least, that Jesus had properly explained a parable. Jesus, perceiving in his spirit that they thus questioned within themselves, said to them, "This containment period has really got me in a weird headspace at the moment."

Translators: **Toby Isaacson, Mat Taylor** and **Darius Tooyserkani**

Matthew 8:5-10

Jesus Heals a Servant

Now when Jesus had entered Capernaum, a centurion who was working from home, zoomed Him, and pled, "Lord, my servant is lying here paralyzed, dreadfully tormented."

And Jesus said to him, "I will come and heal him."

The centurion answered and said, "Lord, I am afraid that we would spread the virus should you come under my roof. But only speak a word, and my servant will be healed. For I am wise and keep my social distance from all. I wash my hands, wear masks and buy lots of sanitiser and cleaning products. I have not succumbed to stock piling toilet paper.

For I also am a man under authority, having soldiers under me. And I say to this one, 'Go,' and he goes; and to another, 'Come,' and he comes; and to my servant, 'Do this,' and he does it."

When Jesus heard it, He marvelled, and said to all those who were in his zoom meeting, "Assuredly, I say to you, I have not found such great faith, not even in Israel!"

Translator: **Othniel Downs**

Matthew 13:3-9; Mark 4:3-9; Luke 8:5-8

The Parable of the Sneezer

"Behold, an asymptomatic carrier went out grocery shopping. As he sneezed, some of the droplets fell on a non-porous surface and the manager came and wiped it down. Some of the virus-laden droplets fell on cardboard packaging, and took hold, but were unable to reproduce."

"Some of the droplets fell on people who washed their hands thoroughly upon returning home, choking out the spread of the virus. But some of the droplets landed on people with poor hygiene who disregarded shelter-in-place, and the virus multiplied thirty times, sixty times and some a hundred times."

Then Jesus said, "Let him who has PPE wear it!"

Translator: **Tim Chase**

Mark 4:21-25; Luke 8:16-18
The toilet roll under a bowl

No one buys loads of toilet rolls and hides them under a bowl or a bed. Instead, they are placed in the toilet roll holder so all can use.

Unless of course, there's panic buying because of a respiratory virus that doesn't actually need toilet paper. In which case, you should buy them and hide them to prevent others judging you for hoarding.

Translator: **John Spencer**

Mt 13:31-32; Mk 4:30-32; Lk 13:18-19
The Parable of the Pandemic

Jesus told them another parable: "The kingdom of the Heaven is like the coronavirus mutated in a bat. Though it is the smallest of all viruses, it spreads and infects every household and causes many to...wait a second...."

Jesus paused before continuing, "I think that was a bad analogy. Let's go with something more neutral like the Kingdom being like a mustard seed."

Translator: **John Spencer**

Matthew 13:44

The Hidden Pallet

Again, the Kingdom of Heaven is like a pallet of toilet paper hidden in the warehouse which a man found, and hid. In his joy, he goes and sells all that he has, and buys that warehouse.

Translator: **Tim Chase**

Matthew 13:45-46

The Toilet Paper of Great Price

Again, the Kingdom of Heaven is like a shopper searching for toilet paper during panic buying. When he discovers the last one in the supermarket, he sells everything he owns to buy it as it was a super-soft 4 ply quilted gold-plated deluxe pack infused with aloe vera.

Translator: **John Spencer**

John 6:1-14

Jesus turns 5 rolls into 5000

Some time after the measures imposed by Caesar Boris, Jesus crossed to the far shores of the Isle of Wight. Due to selfish stockpiling going on, a great crowd of people followed him from the local supermarket (whilst maintaining social distancing) because they saw the signs and wonders that he had performed. Then Jesus went up to the ferry port and sat down with his disciples as the time of the Isle of Wight Festival was near.

When Jesus looked up and saw the great crowd coming toward him, he said to Philip, "Where shall we get toilet paper for these people to use?" He asked this only to test him, for he already had in mind what he was going to do.

Philip answered him, "It would take more than half a year's wages to buy enough toilet paper for each one to have only a single square! And that's at Asda/Walmart essentials pricing and they have no stock at the moment anyway."

Another of his disciples, Andrew, Simon Peter's brother, spoke up, "Here is a boy with a package of double-ply toilet paper. But still how far will they go among so many?"

Jesus said, "Have the people sit down sat exactly two meters/six foot apart from each other (depending on whether they prefer metric or not)." The disciples did so, but still feared that they would be arrested for holding such a large gathering. Then Jesus took the package of toilet paper, gave thanks, and distributed to those who were seated to take as much as they wanted.

When they had all had enough to wipe their behinds, he said to his disciples, "Gather the pieces that are left over and make new rolls from them so that nothing be wasted."

So they gathered them and made another twelve full rolls of toilet paper.

After the people saw the sign Jesus performed, they began to say, "No longer will we go to the store to queue only to find the shelves empty." And many came to faith in Jesus as long as he was able to keep on providing the goods that they felt were essential for them during this crisis.

Translators: **Nathan Ramsden-Lock, John Spencer** and **Richie Richards**

Matthew 22:1-9; Luke 14:15-24
The Great Banquet

Once, there was a man who prepared a wedding banquet for his son and sent out many invitations. When all was ready, he sent his servant to inform the guests that it was time to come. But they all began to make excuses. The first said, 'I apologise, but I can't disobey the government's lockdown.'

Another said, 'I apologise, but our hazmat suits have a leak.'

Still another said, 'I've a fever and need to self-isolate for 14 days.'

The servant reported all this to his master. His master was angry with himself because he totally forgot about the quarantine and told the servant, 'Quickly, go find some tubs to put all this food in so it doesn't go to waste.' But even then, he regretted not buying another chest freezer.

Translator: **John Spencer**

Luke 15:8-10

The Lost Facemask

Suppose a woman has N95 facemasks and loses one. Won't she light a lamp, sweep the house and search every corner of the house until she finds it? And when she finds it, won't she zoom call her friends and neighbours to rejoice with her for she can now go out for groceries?

And won't she place over-reliance on her mask and forget about the gloves, social distancing. and washing her hands and then contract the virus anyway?

And so wouldn't it be better if she had never found the mask in the first place?

Translator: **John Spencer**

Luke 16:19-31
The Rich Man and Lazarus

There once was a rich man who was splendidly protected in a solid gold facemask, and had stockpiles of pasta, toilet roll, and hand sanitiser. A poor, diseased beggar named Lazarus was unable to get to the stores before they sold out of food and healthcare items. He longed to eat whatever might fall from the rich man's table, but the quarantine meant he couldn't get his friends to lay him at the rich man's gate, let alone under the rich man's table.

Then the beggar died of coronavirus and was carried by the angels to be with Abraham. The rich man also died from the virus because, as you know, it doesn't respect class. He ended up in the fires of hell where he looked up and was miffed when he saw Abraham in the distance with Lazarus by his side.

He called out, 'Father Abraham, have mercy. Send Lazarus to me to dip his finger in water and cool my tongue, because I am in agony in this fire and my throat is still not recovered from the coughing.'

But Abraham said, 'Son, you know the quarantine restrictions, besides there is a vast social distancing chasm separating us so that no one can go from here to you even if they wanted to break the lockdown, nor can anyone cross from there to us.'

The rich man said, 'Then send Lazarus to my father's house, for I have five brothers. Let him warn them how no-one is immune to Coronavirus so they can put off joining me here in this place of torment until they eaten, drunk, and been merry.'

But Abraham replied, 'They have the Scriptures which warn them repeatedly about washing and sending infected people outside the camp. They're also are quite clear about what happens to those who live for themselves.'

'No Father Abraham, if someone came back from the dead then my brothers would repent.'

But Abraham said, 'If they saw someone come back from the dead they certainly would make good use of that hoarded toilet paper, but if they don't listen to the government guidelines nor read the word of God then making them poop their pants in shock from seeing Lazarus alive again isn't going to change anything, except maybe the amount of alcohol they consume.'

Translator: **John Spencer**

Luke 18:1-8

Parable of the persistent widow

Jesus told his disciples a parable to show their need to be persistent in queuing and never quit. He said, "There was a supermarket CEO in a town who did not fear God, nor did he care for people. A widow in that town queued every day to get into the store only to be disappointed. So, she berated him saying, 'Grant me a packet of pasta.' At first, the CEO ignored her, but eventually, she got picked up by the news and people on social media started trolling the CEO until he finally caved in.

'I might not fear God nor care for people, but if I don't give this woman pasta, this trolling will drive me insane!'"

Then Jesus said, "If an evil CEO can be worn down like that and produce pasta when there's a shortage, don't you think God will also give pizza to his chosen people who continue to cry out for help whilst in lockdown? He won't put them off, He will answer them quickly. But the question is: will I find that persistent faith when I return or will they just order takeout?"

Translator: **John Spencer**

Luke 18:9-14

The Pharisee and the Tax Collector

Then he told this parable to those who were confident in their own Coronavirus preventative measures and looked down on everyone else.

"Two men went to the Temple to pray, one a Pharisee; the other a tax collector. The Pharisee prayed: 'God, I thank you that I'm not like everyone else, especially not that tax collector more than six foot over there! For I wash my hands twice an hour and give a tenth of all my used toilet paper away. I also report all my neighbours when they break the quarantine requirements.'

But the tax collector stood at a distance, his face in his hands, not daring to look up to Heaven and said, 'God have mercy on me, for I have just touched my face with my hands.'

I tell you that this tax collector rather than the other went home right with God. For the proud shall still catch the virus, but the humble won't be such jerks about it."

Translator: **John Spencer**

Matthew 19:13-15
Jesus and the Children

Then were there brought unto him little children, that he should put his hands on them, and pray: and the disciples rebuked the crowd, for they ignored the chalk marks upon the ground, which James and John had drawn out to show how far people should stand from the Lord.

But Jesus said, "Suffer little children, and forbid them not, to come unto me: for the chalk lines have faded and you really should've used brightly coloured tape, for it doth last longer."

And he laid his hands on the children, and departed thence. Two days later, he developed some mild symptoms and so healed people from home through Zoom chat as he had previously done with the centurion.

Translator: **Michael Richard Bullock**

Luke 19:1-7

Zacchaeus the Tax Collector

Jesus entered Jericho and was passing through. A man was there by the name of Zacchaeus; he was a chief tax collector and was wealthy. He wanted to see who Jesus was, but because of the social distancing he could not risk getting close to the crowd. So he ran ahead and climbed at least six foot up a sycamore-fig tree to see him, since Jesus was coming that way.

When Jesus reached the spot, he looked up and said to him, "Zacchaeus, come down immediately. I must stay at your house today." So he came down at once and welcomed him gladly.

All the people saw this and began to mutter, "He has broken the quarantine guidelines!"

Translator: **John Spencer**

Matthew 18:21-35
The Unmerciful Servant

Then Peter came to Jesus and asked, "Master, how many days should I remain quarantined with my brother Andrew who sins against me? Should it be seven days, the number of perfection?"

Jesus replied, "Not seven days but seventy times seven"

"The Kingdom of Heaven is like a king who decided to prosecute his servants who had been breaching the quarantine restrictions. One of his servants who was brought before him in a zoom meeting had gone outside for 3 hours and mixed with over 50 people.

So the king ordered the man, his wife, children, and all his belongings to be placed in one room for 50 days.

"The man gasped in horror and threw himself at the king's feet via zoom and begged, 'Have mercy on me and I'll make up for my lapse in judgement.' The king took pity on him, released him and forgave him.

After the man had signed off from Zoom, he saw from his window one of his fellow servants buying non-essential from the local store. He phoned him and shouted, 'You broke the lockdown I'm going to ensure the police know!'

The fellow servant begged, 'Have mercy on me, and I'll only ever purchase food and medicine from now on.' But the man refused and had his fellow servant put in jail. When the other servants saw the video of this on social media, they were outraged and told the king everything (after they had reposted the video to stir up outrage).

"The king summoned the servant for a virtual meeting and said, 'You wicked servant! I forgave you mixing with over 50 people when you begged for mercy. Shouldn't you have had mercy on your fellow servant just as I had mercy on you?'

"The king was so angry that he ordered the man to be placed in lockdown with all his family in just one room with no internet and with a game of monopoly.

"So too shall my heavenly father treat you if you refuse to stay quarantined with your family.

Translator: **John Spencer**

Matthew 18:20

Gathering Together

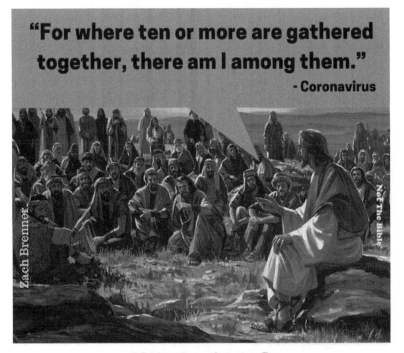

"For where ten or more are gathered together, there am I among them."

- Coronavirus

Matt 18:20 (sort of)

Translator: **Zach Brenner**

Luke 22

The Last Supper

Then came the day of Unleavened Bread on which the supermarkets had sold out of every other kind. Jesus emailed Peter and John, saying, "Go and make preparations for us to eat the Passover."

"Where do you want us to prepare for it?" they asked.

He replied, "As you surf online, you will see an ad for an online meeting app. Click on it and follow the instructions on the webpage, and say to the owner of the webpage, 'The Teacher asks: What is the code for the meeting room, where I may eat the Passover with my disciples?' He will give you an 11 figure code for a large upper zoom. Make preparations there."

They left and found things just as Jesus had told them. So they prepared the Passover.

The Last Supper
in the Upper Zoom

When the hour came, Jesus and his apostles reclined on their sofas at home. And he said to them, "I have eagerly desired to eat this Passover with you but the lockdown has still not been lifted."

After taking his grape soda and Doritos, he gave thanks and said, "Now take whatever you have found in the fridge and eat and drink it. For I tell you we will not have proper food again until the shortages end."

But a dispute arose among them as to which of them was considered to be greatest and so Jesus put them all on mute until they had finished arguing.

Translator: **John Spencer**

Acts 1:6-8

Jesus taken up to Heaven

When they gathered together on Zoom, they asked Jesus, "Leader, is this the time you are going to cleanse the internet?" He said to them, "It is not for you to know the date or timeline the Father has planned. But you will receive Theology degrees when the Student Debt has come upon you, and you will be my witnesses on Facebook and in all Forums and Chatrooms, and to the ends of the internet. So, go therefore to all the corners of the web and quote theology to all online trolls and then the end will come.

After he said this, he was taken from their sight as the connection dropped and Jesus was uploaded to the cloud.

Translators: **The Satire Bible** and **John Spencer**.

Romans – Hebrews
Paul's Letters

Paul, servant of Christ, set apart for the gospel of God – set apart by social distancing – conveyed a message to the Christians of the Roman world:

To Rome, Paul sent a letter, though its delivery was delayed due to a reduced postal service, as well as the fact the postman was not quite sure where in Rome to deliver it. Eventually he found the house, and left the letter outside the front door, after banging on the door with a long pole and running away.

Therein the Romans read a letter of great encouragement: that they need not be ashamed of their faith, and that these small house-churches should perhaps put up something in their windows, like a rainbow or a cross or a picture of a heart made with fingers, which isn't as creepy as it first sounds.

Paul wrote to them that they were justified by faith, not works, though works be good, and God blesses those who do them, especially on the front line. For the other workers, well, the wages of sin currently stood at a rate of 80% if furloughed.

Paul decided to send another message, to the people of Corinth. As he wanted his message to reach them more quickly and reliably, he tried a Zoom call. He sent them the meeting ID, and when the people of Corinth had arranged their books to make a nice background, the call went ahead and Paul conveyed his message. He told them love is kind, and love is patient, and he too was kind and patient when he realised they had accidentally pressed 'mute' while trying to reply to him, and were pointing the camera at the ceiling. The Corinthians noted down Paul's words and thought they'd be good at future weddings, when they were allowed to have them again.

The call was briefly cut off, and thus Paul made a second Zoom call to the Corinthians.

Then Paul wanted to send a message to the Galatians, so he thought he'd try FaceTime, to see if the connection was more reliable. He told the Galatians that the fruit of the Spirit was love, joy, peace, patience, kindness, goodness, faithfulness, but that fruit was also an Apple as that's how both sides connected.

Then Paul sent a message to the Ephesians, this time via WhatsApp encouraging them to wear the PPE of God.

Paul returned to his webcam for a message to the Philippians, telling them not to be anxious. And the Philippians replied,

"That's all very well, but this Skype connection is being sent via 3G." So Paul reassured them, that we can do all things through him who gives us strength, which is Christ Jesus, and not Joe Wicks, though they can look similar in a certain light due to the haircut.

To the Colossians, Paul spoke via livestream, and they heard the words in chunks because Colossae was a backwater town lacking high-speed broadband.

To the Thessalonians, Paul sent two messages, urging them to build each other up and encourage one another, which was and is a most important message in times of crisis. And the Thessalonians did shopping for each other, and picked up prescriptions, and even exchanged goods and pleasantries with the Colossians and Galatians, who they didn't really get on with as they heard Paul had sent messages to the others first and they were a bit jealous.

Paul wanted to reach his friend Timothy, but due to self-isolation (in prison) that proved tricky. So they had a great couple of Houseparty sessions, where they played games, and talked about how scripture is God-breathed, and spoke of the role of women in the church, though the connection was dodgy so it may have cut out then and missed some important clarification.

With Titus, Philemon, and the Hebrews, Paul had a great Watch Party, for although he was stuck in prison for much of this, so was everyone else, in a way. The main thing was that they kept communicating, and didn't let a few annoying walls and a bit of temporary distance get in the way of being a community together.

Translator: **Paul Kerensa**

Romans 8:38-39

More than conquerors

In all things we are more than conquerors through him who loved us. For I am convinced that neither death nor life, neither angels nor demons, neither the present nor the future, nor any powers, neither height nor depth, nor anything else in all creation, will be able to separate us from the love of God that is in Christ Jesus our Lord.

Except, of course, for the Coronavirus. That's just too hard for God's love to reach through. In which case, you must hide yourself away and rely on stockpiling to save you.

Translator: **John Spencer**

1 Corinthians 7:36

Dating honourably

Christian dating during the Coronavirus

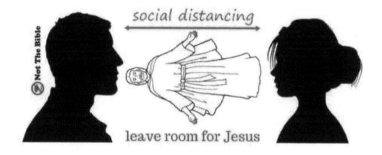

Translator: **John Spencer**

Ephesians 6:13-18

The ~~Armour~~ PPE of God

Therefore put on the ESSENTIAL OILS of KAREN, so that when the day of evil comes, you may be able to stand your ground, and after you have done everything, to stand.

Stand firm then, with the FIRST AID KIT of truth buckled around your waist, with the HAZMAT SUIT of righteousness in place,

And with your feet fitted with the readiness to phone the police when someone breaks the gospel of lockdown.

In addition to all this, take up the LYSOL of faith, with which you can extinguish all the flaming COUGHS AND SNEEZES of the evil one.

Take the MEDICAL MASK of salvation and the PURELL of the Spirit, which is the word of God.

And SPRAY WINDEX in the Spirit on all occasions with all kinds of DISINFECTANTS and requests. With this in mind, be alert and always keep on spraying all the Lord's people.

Translator: **Darius Tooyserkani**

Philippians 4:7

The peace of God

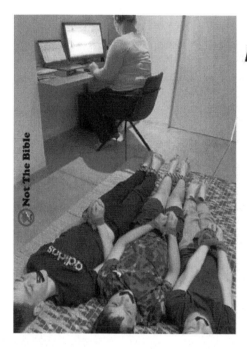

And the peace of God, which surpasses all understanding, will guard your hearts and your minds in Christ Jesus.

Phil 4:7 (sort of)

Translator: **John Spencer**

Philippians 4:18
Gifts for the Ministry

HOW CHURCHES COLLECT TITHES
DURING CORONAVIRUS LIVESTREAMS

Translator: **John Spencer**

2 Corinthians 13:12

Paul signs off his letters

~~Great one another with a holy kiss~~

Greet one another with a respectful nod, by the hand sanitiser station, and a few feet apart from one another.

Translator: **Sam Allberry**

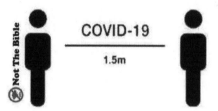

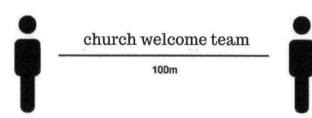

1 Timothy 3:2

Social distancing for bishops

Hebrews 10:25
Meeting together

Churches pre-COVID **Churches post-COVID**

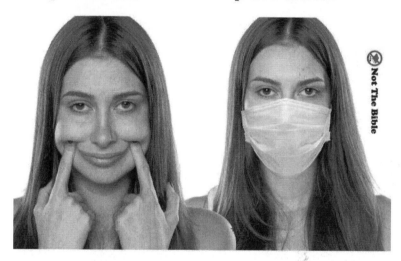

metapohorical mask   literal mask

Translator: **John Spencer**

Hebrews 12:1-2

Fix your eyes

Therefore, since we are surrounded by such great cases of COVID-19, let us also lay aside going outside, and all our work which clings so close, and let us shelter-in-place with endurance the timeframe that is set before us, looking to the CDC, the authority and tester of this virus, who for the sake of the greater good only tests the seriously ill, despising the economic downturn, and is seated at the right hand of the administration.

Translator: **The Satire Bible**

James 2:14-17

Faith and deeds

What good is it, my brothers, if a man claims to have faith but has no deeds? Can such faith save him? Suppose a brother or sister is without clothes and daily food due to the lockdown. If one of you says to him, "Go, I wish you well; keep warm and well fed," but does nothing about his physical needs, what good is it? In the same way, faith by itself, if it is not accompanied by action, is dead.

Make sure to exercise your faith by asking the government to do more for those in need as it's their job to look after those struggling in these times.

Translator: **John Spencer**

James 4:8

Wash your hands, you sinners

When experts say to wash your hands for the length of a song but you only listen to Hillsong Live

Translator: **Brady Cox**

Revelation 3:14-22

Email to the Church in Laodicea

"To the angel of the church in Laodicea email the following:

These are the words of the CEO of Heaven, the ruler of God's creation.

I wanted to take the time to let you know what steps we are taking during this Coronavirus crisis to ensure the safety of our angels and all our ~~customers~~ disciples like you.

Firstly, we have installed a six-foot distancing rule between those queuing to enter the throne room of heaven. Secondly, we have put restrictions on some prayer requests to prevent immature Christians stockpiling prayers for protection and leaving some without a hedge of protections. Thirdly, we are currently recruiting more angels to help with the delivery of God's blessing at this time, while visits to the throne room are experiencing high demand.

Here I am! I stand at the door and knock. If anyone hears my voice and opens the door, I will chastise them for breaking the quarantine restrictions. Those whom I love I rebuke and discipline, so be earnest, and repent.

To him who overcomes the lock down, I will give the right to sit on the golden throne with quality 4 ply quilted toilet paper."

Translator: **John Spencer**

Revelation 20:1-5
A new Heaven and Earth

Then I saw a new heaven and a new earth, for the first heaven and first earth had passed away, and there no longer any viruses.

And I heard a loud voice from throne saying, "Now the dwelling of God is with men, and he will live with them for there is no more social distancing. He will remove every mask from their face and every glove from their hands. There will be no more sneezing, face touching, or zoom meetings, for the old order has passed away."

He who was seated on the throne said, "Behold! I am making everything new! He who overcomes the quarantine will inherit all this, and I will be his God and he will be my son."

Translator: John Spencer

Want to help more?

Thank you so much for purchasing this book to raise money for charities working with those in need.

You could help us raise more money by recommending it to your friends and leaving a review of this book on Amazon or Goodreads to encourage others to buy it.

We're keeping no money for ourselves and we have funded its production costs out of our own pocket, so every penny raised will go direct to the charities listed at the front of the book.

COVID Christian News Satire

50 COVID satirical news articles from **The Salty Cee** comedy team, including:

- Popular bacon face mask "not effective protection" against Coronavirus

- N95 face mask arrested for hate crime!

- Church Gives Away Toilet roll to Increase Streamed Service Attendance.

- 5 second rule to be reduced due to Coronavirus fears

- Jehovah's Witnesses switch to carrier pigeons

The Salty Cee: more salty than the Dead Sea

How this book came about

David S Smith wrote Proverbs 31 as the original translation for the Coronavirus Version Bible as an article for **The Salty Cee** Christian Satirical News website.

John Spencer, editor of that site, thought the idea was so good that we should write a whole Coronavirus Version Bible and give the money to charities supporting people during this crisis.

After quickly realising that might be a bit too much to complete this in a time frame that would raise money when it's most needed, John put out the call for others to help out.

Scott Norris, a regular Salty Cee contributor was first to answer, followed by a The Church News Headlines, a fellow Christian satire Twitter account.

The Super God Comedy Squad of British Christian comedians were next to throw their support behind it.

Finally, the many followers of The Salty Cee website and Not the Bible meme page contributed so many great ideas that made this book happen so much faster than we could ever have dreamed possible.

List of Contributors

The Salty Cee contributors

John Spencer

Scott Norris

David S Smith

Othniel Downs

Richie Richards

Super God Comedy Squad contributors

Michael Richard Bullock

Nathan Ramsden-Lock

Paul Kerensa

Tim Hill

Israel Matthews

Pete Hawkins

Toby Isaacson

Mat Taylor

Bentley Browning

Other accounts

The Satire Bible

The Church Curmudgeon

The Church News Headlines

Sam Allberry

Not the Bible meme page followers

Tim Chase

Darius Tooyserkani

Robbie Squier

Mike Sartoris

Zach Brenner

Filbert Joshua

Alan Findlay

Cheryl Booker

Brady Cox

James Grigsby

Lynsey Gilmour

Zoey Granitz

Rachel Louise

Patience Domowski

Other books by the authors

John Spencer

Christian Parody Titles
40 Biblical Ways to Annoy Your Spouse
Because everyone needs some biblical help to justify their annoying habits to their spouse

Not the Christmas Story: A Comedic Christmas Caper
"Fear not: for, behold, I bring you good tidings of great laughter, which shall be to all purchasers of this book."

Not the Bible Titles
Different takes on the Bible to make you laugh and think.

Not the Parables of Jesus

More Not the Parables of Jesus

Not the Parable of the Good Samaritan

Still More Not the Parables of Jesus

Not the Christmas Story Vol 1 *(with devotional)*

Christian Satirical News Titles
The Best of the Salty Cee Vol 1 & Vol 2
Christian News Satire more salty than the Dead Sea.

Paul Kerensa

Award-winning writer of TV, radio, books and his own stand-up comedy.

Noah's Car Park Ark: A Multi-Storey Story

So a Comedian Walks into Church

Hark! The Biography of Christmas

What are they doing down there?

Church Curmudgeon

The Internet's most infamous purveyor of fine vintage Christian whines.

Then Tweets My Soul

Sam Allberry

Writer, pastor, consumer of Thai food and bestselling author.

Why does God care who I sleep with?

7 Myths about Singleness

Connected

Made in the USA
Columbia, SC
19 August 2022

65651176R00098